McDougal Littell
MATH
Course 2

Larson   Boswell   Kanold   Stiff

Practice Workbook

**The Practice Workbook provides additional practice
for every lesson in the textbook. The workbook covers
essential vocabulary, skills, and problem solving.
Space is provided for students to show their work.**

McDougal Littell
A DIVISION OF HOUGHTON MIFFLIN COMPANY
Evanston, Illinois • Boston • Dallas

Contents

Name _____ Date _____

Practice

For use with pages 3-7

Describe the pattern. Then write the next three numbers.

1. 1, 3, 9, 27, . . .   **2.** 4, 10, 16, 22, . . .   **3.** 21, 19, 17, 15, . . .

4. 3, 12, 48, 192, . . .   **5.** 6400, 3200, 1600, 800, . . .   **6.** 4, 20, 100, 500, . . .

7. Every four years, the month of February has 29 days instead of 28 days. The last leap year occurred in 2000. When will the next four leap years occur?

Describe the pattern. Then draw the next figure.

8.

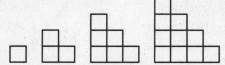

9.

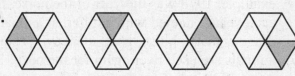

10. The owner's manual for your car states that you should have the oil changed every 3750 miles. If you started driving the car at 0 miles, when will the first five oil changes occur? Describe the pattern for the oil changes.

Describe the pattern. Then write the next three letters.

11. A, D, G, J, . . .   **12.** Z, X, V, T, . . .   **13.** A, E, I, M, . . .

Name _____ Date _____

Practice

For use with pages 3–7

Describe the pattern. Then draw the next figure.

14.    15.

16. In the Chinese calendar, each year is named as an animal. For example, 1978 was the year of the horse. During a 12-year period, each year is named with a different animal (rat, ox, tiger, rabbit, dragon, snake, horse, goat, monkey, rooster, dog, and pig). Then the animals are used over again for the next 12 years in the same order. After 1978, what are the next five years of the horse? Describe the pattern you used to answer the question.

17. A sweater is decorated with the Southwestern-inspired design shown below. Draw the next three figures that will continue the pattern.

Name _____ Date _____

Practice

For use with pages 8–11

Evaluate the expression for the given value of the variable.

1. $p + 13$ when $p = 8$

2. $23 - x$ when $x = 6$

3. $13y$ when $y = 7$

4. $\dfrac{b}{5}$ when $b = 75$

5. $m - 4$ when $m = 33$

6. $\dfrac{81}{a}$ when $a = 3$

7. Your part-time summer job pays $7 per hour. To find the amount of money you can earn in one week, you can evaluate the expression $7h$, where h is the number of hours you work during the week. If you work 15 hours your first week, how much money do you earn for the week?

8. To find the number of calories from protein in a serving of food, you can evaluate the expression $4g$, where g is the number of grams of protein in a serving. If a serving of nuts contains 12 grams of protein, how many calories from protein are in the serving?

Name _____ Date _____

Practice

For use with pages 8–11

Evaluate the expression when $a = 3$, $b = 8$, $m = 24$, and $q = 35$.

9. $b + q$

10. am

11. $q - m$

12. $\dfrac{m}{b}$

13. $m - b$

14. $a + q$

15. During the winter, weather forecasters give the actual outdoor temperature and the "wind chill" temperature. This is because the blowing wind can make it feel colder than it actually is. The expression $a - w$, where w is the wind chill temperature and a is the actual temperature, can be used to find how many degrees colder it feels outside when the wind is blowing. If the actual temperature is 35° F and the wind chill temperature is 16° F, how many degrees colder does it feel because of the wind?

16. The Pennsylvania Turnpike is a roadway that spans approximately 528 miles across the entire state. To find how long it will take you to drive across the state on the turnpike, you can evaluate the expression $\dfrac{L}{r}$, where L is the length of the Pennsylvania Turnpike and r is your driving speed. If you maintain a driving speed of 66 miles per hour, how many hours will it take you to drive across the state?

17. Which two expressions are the same?

A. $\dfrac{a}{b}$

B. $a - b$

C. $a \div b$

D. $\dfrac{b}{a}$

Name _____ Date _____

Practice

For use with pages 13–16

Write the power in words.

1. 3^8

2. 9^4

3. y^5

Write the product as a power.

4. $2 \cdot 2 \cdot 2 \cdot 2 \cdot 2 \cdot 2$

5. $13 \cdot 13 \cdot 13$

6. $6 \cdot 6 \cdot 6 \cdot 6$

7. $r \cdot r \cdot r$

8. $a \cdot a \cdot a \cdot a \cdot a \cdot a \cdot a$

9. $t \cdot t \cdot t \cdot t$

Evaluate the power.

10. 2^5

11. 7^4

12. 10^3

13. 3^5

14. 6^3

15. 1^4

Name _____ Date _____

Practice

For use with pages 13–16

Evaluate the expression for the given value of the variable.

16. y^2 when $y = 12$ **17.** b^5 when $b = 4$ **18.** w^3 when $w = 15$

19. v^6 when $v = 3$ **20.** s^4 when $s = 10$ **21.** m^8 when $m = 2$

Write the number as a power.

22. 25   **23.** 121   **24.** 64

25. Write each number in the pattern as a power: 1, 4, 9, 16, 25, . . .

26. Computers store information in units called bits and bytes. A kilobyte is 2^{10} bytes. Evaluate the power to find the number of bytes in a kilobyte.

27. In the metric system of weight, there are 1000 milligrams in one gram. Write the number of milligrams in one gram as a power.

28. The solid figure below is called a cube and is made of blocks that are all the same size. How many blocks make up the cube? Write the number of blocks that make up the cube as a power.

Name _____ Date _____

Practice

For use with pages 17–22

Evaluate the expression.

1. $10 + 6 \cdot 8$

2. $35 - 20 \div 5$

3. $18(11 - 6)$

4. $28 \div (16 - 9)$

5. $\dfrac{14 + 10}{7 - 4}$

6. $33 \div (3^2 + 2)$

7. $5(7 + 5)^2$

8. $(5 - 3)^3 + 12 \div 4$

9. $11(8 + 3^2) - 15$

Evaluate the expression when $x = 4$, $y = 12$, and $z = 9$.

10. $3xy - 7$

11. $3x^2 + y$

12. $\dfrac{5y}{x}$

13. $4z^2 - x$

14. $\dfrac{y - z}{3}$

15. $(y - x)^2 + 14$

16. $\dfrac{x + y}{z - 5}$

17. $(x^2 - y)(z + 4)$

18. $36 \div z - x$

Name _____ Date _____

Practice

For use with pages 17–22

Match the given expression with the expression that has the same value.

19. $36 - 5^2 + 7$ **A.** $2^2 \cdot 8 - 10$

20. $27 - 2 \cdot 4 + 3$ **B.** $(4^2 + 38) \div 3$

21. $12(8 - 3)$ **C.** $(5 + 3)^2 - 4$

22. Your local phone company offers DSL service for connecting to the Internet. There is a one-time $100 hookup fee and monthly charges are $40 for the service. Write and evaluate an expression to find the cost of getting DSL service for the first year.

23. At the beginning of the workday, a cashier will start out with money in his or her cash register so that change can be made. A cash register contains 50 one-dollar bills, 30 five-dollar bills, and 8 ten-dollar bills. Write and evaluate an expression that will give you the total amount of money in the cash register.

Practice

For use with pages 25–30

Tell whether the given value of the variable is a solution of the equation.

1. $7x = 42; x = 6$ **2.** $7 + a = 19; a = 12$ **3.** $z \div 4 = 6; z = 2$

4. $b - 16 = 28; b = 34$ **5.** $n + 8 = 21; n = 13$ **6.** $33 - y = 18; y = 25$

Match the equation with the corresponding question. Then solve.

7. $6x = 48$ **A.** 6 plus what number equals 48?

8. $x \div 6 = 8$ **B.** What number divided by 6 equals 8?

9. $6 + x = 48$ **C.** 6 times what number equals 48?

10. $\dfrac{48}{x} = 6$ **D.** 48 divided by what number equals 6?

Solve the equation using mental math.

11. $b + 15 = 23$ **12.** $25 - x = 16$ **13.** $40 \div a = 8$

14. $7m = 56$ **15.** $y \div 4 = 10$ **16.** $p - 12 = 7$

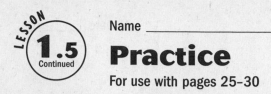

Name _____ Date _____

Practice

For use with pages 25–30

Use the formula for distance to find the unknown value.

17. $d = 100$ miles, $r =$ ____, $t = 5$ hours

18. $d = 360$ kilometers, $r = 40$ kilometers per hour, $t =$ ____

19. $d = 420$ miles, $r =$ ____, $t = 7$ hours

20. The slowest flying bird in the world flies at a speed of 5 miles per hour. How long does it take for the bird to fly 15 miles?

21. Telescopes are described by their f/number. The f/number is given by the equation $f = F \div D$, where f is the f/number, F is the focal length of the telescope, and D is the width of the telescope lens. Use the f/number equation to find the focal length (in inches) of a telescope with a 10-inch wide lens and an f/number of 9.

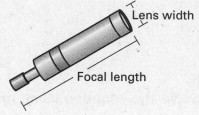

Lens width

Focal length

22. Two scales used for measuring temperature are the Kelvin scale and the Celsius scale. A temperature in degrees Kelvin is about 273 degrees greater than a temperature in degrees Celsius. Solve the equation $300 = C + 273$ to find the temperature in degrees Celsius that is the same as 300 degrees Kelvin.

Name _____ Date _____

Practice

For use with pages 32–36

Match the figure with its area or perimeter.

1.

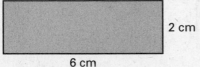

2 cm

6 cm

2.

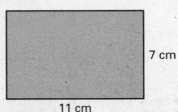

7 cm

11 cm

3.

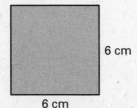

6 cm

6 cm

4.

3 cm

3 cm

A. 12 centimeters

B. 12 square centimeters

C. 36 centimeters

D. 36 square centimeters

Find the perimeter and the area of the rectangle or square with the given dimensions.

5. $\ell = 11$ inches, $w = 5$ inches

6. $s = 4$ meters

7. $s = 10$ millimeters

8. $\ell = 13$ feet, $w = 2$ feet

9. $\ell = 8$ centimeters, $w = 7$ centimeters

10. $s = 7$ inches

11. $s = 3$ meters

12. $\ell = 12$ yards, $w = 6$ yards

Name _____ Date _____

Practice

For use with pages 32–36

13. Which two rectangles with the given length and width have the same area?

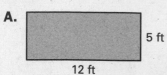

A.   B.

5 ft   5 ft

12 ft   10 ft

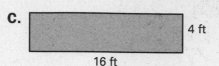

C.   D.

4 ft   2 ft

16 ft   30 ft

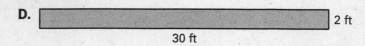

14. A hand-held video game has a screen that is about 61 millimeters long and 41 millimeters wide. What is the perimeter and the area of the screen?

15. Measure the sides of the rectangle to the nearest centimeter. Use your measurements to find the perimeter and the area of the rectangle.

Name _____ Date _____

Practice

For use with pages 37–41

1. Describe and correct the error made in solving the following problem.

You are ordering pizza for a party. One pizza serves 8 people. You expect that there will be 35 people at the party. How many pizzas should you order?

$$\begin{array}{r} 4 \text{ R3} \\ 8\overline{)35} \\ \underline{32} \\ 3 \end{array}$$

You need to order 4 pizzas.

2. Farmers typically do not plant the same crop in the same plot of soil season after season. For each upcoming season, the farmer will switch positions of crops from the previous season to grow healthier plants. This is called crop rotation. The tables below show the rotation of crops for three seasons. If you continue the pattern, how many seasons will it take for the crops to be in the positions they were in the first season?

Season 1		
Beans	Potatoes	Lettuce
Cabbage	Spinach	Carrots

Season 2		
Cabbage	Beans	Potatoes
Spinach	Carrots	Lettuce

Season 3		
Spinach	Cabbage	Beans
Carrots	Lettuce	Potatoes

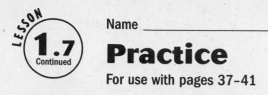

Practice

For use with pages 37–41

3. You have $100 to spend on a new outfit. You spend $25 on shoes and you still need pants and a shirt. You find 3 pants and 2 shirts that you like. The prices for the items are shown in the table. Which combinations of pants and a shirt could you buy with the money you have left?

Item	Price
Tan pants	$48
Navy pants	$34
Black pants	$42
Striped shirt	$38
Solid shirt	$32

4. A computer screen is divided into little squares called pixels. The number of pixels on the screen is called the monitor resolution. A common monitor resolution is 640 × 480, which means that there are 640 pixels along the length of the screen and 480 pixels along the width of the screen. Another common monitor resolution is 800 × 600. How many pixels is the computer screen divided into with each resolution? Which resolution uses more pixels and how many more pixels does it use?

5. A pizza shop offers five different toppings (pepperoni (R), onions (O), peppers (P), sausage (S), and mushrooms (M)) for its pizzas. How many different pizzas can be created using three different toppings? What are the combinations of the toppings?

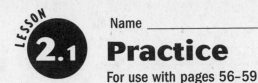
Practice

For use with pages 56–59

Match the decimal with its verbal description.

1. 4.059   **A.** four and fifty-nine hundredths

2. 4.59   **B.** forty and fifty-nine hundredths

3. 45.09   **C.** forty-five and nine hundredths

4. 40.59   **D.** four and fifty-nine thousandths

Complete the statement using <, >, or =.

5. 5.6 _____ 6.5   **6.** 3.48 _____ 3.84

7. 8.52 _____ 8.2   **8.** 18.045 _____ 18.054

9. 6.480 _____ 6.48   **10.** 4.203 _____ 4.302

Order the numbers from least to greatest.

11. 2.4, 1.8, 2.1, 1.2   **12.** 2.6, 3.5, 2.1, 3.0

13. 2.014, 2.402, 2.011, 2.303   **14.** 1.109, 1.910, 1.119, 1.019

15. 8.3, 8.08, 8.74, 8.9   **16.** 3.45, 5.43, 3.5, 4.53

Name _____ Date _____

Practice

For use with pages 56–59

Round the decimal as specified.

17. 18.4 (nearest one)

18. 14.06 (nearest tenth)

19. 25.0096 (nearest thousandth)

20. 6.785 (nearest hundredth)

21. 19.54 (nearest one)

22. 5.006 (nearest tenth)

23. The table shows the difference in feet between high tide and low tide for selected cities along the Atlantic Ocean and the Gulf of Mexico. Order the differences from least to greatest.

City	Difference Between High Tide and Low Tide
Baltimore, MD	1.67 feet
Galveston, TX	1.42 feet
Key West, FL	1.83 feet
Mobile, AL	1.5 feet

24. The Unites States won the women's 400-meter relay in the 1984, 1988, 1992, and 1996 Summer Olympics with times of 41.65 seconds, 41.98 seconds, 42.11 seconds, and 41.95 seconds, respectively. Order the winning times from greatest to least.

Name _____ Date _____

Practice
For use with pages 60-65

Find the sum or difference. Use estimation to check your answer.

1. $12.5 + 3.7$

2. $54.6 + 2.765$

3. $35.4 - 8.9$

4. $142.6 - 37.42$

5. $0.54 + 13.77$

6. $94.32 + 14.829$

7. $67.312 - 5.47$

8. $20.27 - 5.79$

9. $8.215 + 104.56$

Fill in the missing digit.

10.
$$\begin{array}{r} 8.76 \\ + 2.9? \\ \hline 11.71 \end{array}$$

11.
$$\begin{array}{r} 37.25 \\ + 84.?6 \\ \hline 121.61 \end{array}$$

12.
$$\begin{array}{r} 24.75 \\ - 1?.48 \\ \hline 8.27 \end{array}$$

Evaluate the expression when $x = 39.6$ and $y = 14.65$.

13. $12.7 + y$

14. $y - 5.9$

15. $x + y$

16. $x - y$

17. $y - 2.73 + x$

18. $27 - y + x$

Name _____ Date _____

Practice

For use with pages 60–65

Estimate the sum or difference using front-end estimation.

19. $2.84 + 3.21$

20. $12.62 + 9.34$

21. $10.85 - 5.19$

22. $2.77 + 4 + 13.25$

23. $6.04 + 18.85 + 10.25$

24. $8.88 - 3.2$

Evaluate the expression.

25. $347.4 + 2.29 + 14$

26. $79 - 2.304 - 16.7$

27. $65.84 - 7.013 + 14.6$

28. A quarter horse has a top running speed of 47.5 miles per hour and a greyhound has a top running speed of 39.35 miles per hour. How much faster than the greyhound can the quarter horse run?

29. During the 1880s, the average temperature of Earth was 56.65 degrees Fahrenheit. During the 1980s, the average temperature of Earth was 57.36 degrees Fahrenheit. How much warmer was Earth's average temperature in the 1980s than in the 1880s?

30. You are mailing a 4-pound package, an 8-pound package, and a 9-pound package to another city. It will cost $4.86 to mail the 4-pound package, $5.98 to mail the 8-pound package, and $6.11 to mail the 9-pound package. Use front-end estimation to estimate how much it will cost you to mail all three packages.

Name _____ Date _____

Practice

For use with pages 66–70

Find the product. Then check that your answer is reasonable.

1. 4.1×3.5

2. 7.6×2.3

3. 0.4×0.04

4. 0.08×7

5. 0.14×0.85

6. 2.01×3.14

7. 6.3×4.005

8. 0.86×5.041

9. 0.004×0.057

Estimate the product.

10. 7.41×82.3

11. 0.46×3.1

12. 0.15×6.72

Find the area of the rectangle.

13. $\ell = 6.2$ mm, $w = 5$ mm

14. $\ell = 21.6$ yd, $w = 12$ yd

15. $\ell = 0.25$ in., $w = 0.4$ in.

16. Find the perimeter of the square.

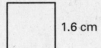

1.6 cm

Name _____ Date _____

Practice

For use with pages 66–70

17. Describe and correct the error in finding the product of 4.02 and 4.02.

$$
\begin{array}{r}
4.02 \\
\times\ 4.02 \\
\hline
8\ 04 \\
1608\ 0 \\
\hline
1616.04
\end{array}
$$

Evaluate the expression when $a = 4.23$ and $b = 6.04$.

18. $3.5a$ **19.** $27.5b$ **20.** ab

21. A gallon of gasoline at the local gas station costs $1.35. If you put 8 gallons of gasoline in your car, how much will it cost you?

22. A tennis court is 23.77 meters long and 8.23 meters wide. Find the area of the tennis court. Round your answer to the nearest hundredth.

23. In 2000, the average annual salary for a person living in Boulder, Colorado was about 1.009 times the average annual salary for a person living in Seattle, Washington. If the average annual salary in Seattle was $45,171, what was the average annual salary in Boulder? Round your answer to the nearest dollar.

Name _____ Date _____

Practice

For use with pages 71–76

Find the quotient. Then check your answer.

1. $300.3 \div 42$

2. $12 \div 2.4$

3. $0.156 \div 1.2$

4. $1.89 \div 3.6$

5. $4.064 \div 2.54$

6. $3.4 \div 1.36$

7. $8.91 \div 16.2$

8. $25.3 \div 101.2$

9. $45.072 \div 125.2$

10. Which two quotients are equal? Explain your reasoning.

A. $3.84 \div 2.56$ **B.** $384 \div 25.6$ **C.** $3.84 \div 25.6$ **D.** $38.4 \div 2.56$

11. Write a quotient that gives the same answer as $4.65 \div 0.12$.

Use compatible numbers to estimate the quotient.

12. $122.56 \div 2.98$

13. $1404.59 \div 73.6$

14. $378.5 \div 61.8$

Find the quotient. Round your answer to the nearest hundredth.

15. $0.347 \div 8$

16. $25 \div 3.7$

17. $11.02 \div 4.25$

18. $9.88 \div 4.7$

19. $12.5 \div 0.78$

20. $61.213 \div 5.6$

Name _____ Date _____

Practice

For use with pages 71–76

Evaluate the expression when $x = 2.5$ and $z = 19.5$.

21. $43.875 \div x + z$ **22.** $\dfrac{z}{x} - 0.23$ **23.** $xz - 2.25$

24. In 1996, Michael Johnson broke the world record for the men's 200-meter run. His record-breaking time was 19.32 seconds. What was Michael Johnson's running speed? Round your answer to the nearest hundredth.

25. The local store has a sale on camera film. If a package containing 5 rolls of film costs $8.99, what is the cost of one roll of film? Round your answer to the nearest cent.

26. You can find the population density for a region, in people per square mile, by dividing the population of the region by the region's area. The area of Long Beach, California is 50.4 square miles. In 2000, Long Beach's population was 461,522. What was the population density of Long Beach in 2000? Round your answer to the nearest tenth.

Name _____ Date _____

Practice

For use with pages 78–81

1. Describe and correct the error in writing the number 81,700,000 in scientific notation.

Standard form	**Product form**	**Scientific notation**
81,700,000	$81.7 \times 100,000$	81.7×10^5

Write the number in scientific notation.

2. 87,300   **3.** 45,600,000   **4.** 91,000,000

5. 437   **6.** 135,000,000   **7.** 1405.6

Write the number in standard form.

8. 8.6×10^5 **9.** 4.15×10^3 **10.** 7×10^4

11. 6.205×10^8 **12.** 1.2654×10^3 **13.** 9.06×10^7

Complete the statement using <, >, or = .

14. 4.15×10^{16} _____ 3.25×10^{18}

15. 2.817×10^{20} _____ 9.2×10^{20}

16. 5.1×10^7 _____ 51,000,000

Name _____ Date _____

Practice

For use with pages 78–81

Order the numbers from least to greatest.

17. 8.015×10^3 8.15×10^2 8.2×10^4 8.07×10^3

18. 4.41×10^5 6.21×10^4 4.2×10^5 5.17×10^6

19. 5.3×10^3 5.02×10^4 6.4×10^4 6.13×10^3

Find the missing digit(s).

20. $72,000 = 7.2 \times 10^{-}$

21. $1,4 \_\_ 0,000 = 1.\_\_ 5 \times 10^6$

22. $8 \_\_,300,000 = \_\_.23 \times 10^7$

23. In 2000, the top attendance at an amusement park in the world was 16,507,000 people. Write the number of people in scientific notation.

24. In 2000, an estimated 1.25×10^8 people spoke Japanese as their first language and an estimated 7.7×10^7 people spoke Wu Chinese as their first language. In 2000, which language had more speakers?

25. In 2000, an estimated 1.664×10^8 dollars in 1000-dollar bills were in circulation. How many 1000-dollar bills were in circulation in 2000?

Name _____ Date _____

Practice

For use with pages 84–89

Estimate the length of the object. Then measure the object using a metric ruler.

1. your thumb   **2.** your pencil   **3.** a notebook

4. Determine the mass of the object by reading the scale.

5. Determine how much liquid is in the measuring cup.

Complete the statement with the appropriate metric unit.

6. A flamingo is 120 _____ tall.

7. The mass of a softball is 177 _____.

8. A swimming pool contains 20,000 _____ of water.

9. The Golden Gate bridge is 1280 _____ long.

10. The mass of an elephant is 6000 _____.

11. A container of juice holds 1893 _____.

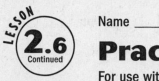
Practice

For use with pages 84–89

Choose the letter of the most reasonable measurement.

12. The length of a baseball bat is _____.

  A. 500 mm

  B. 107 cm

  C. 2000 cm

  D. 3 m

13. The mass of an orange is _____.

  A. 30 g

  B. 700 mg

  C. 1.5 kg

  D. 131 g

14. The capacity of a paint can is _____.

  A. 1200 mL

  B. 3 L

  C. 10 L

  D. 5 kL

Complete the statement using 1.3, 13, or 130.

15. A bar of soap has a mass of about _____ grams.

16. A book has a mass of about _____ kilograms.

17. Five crackers have a mass of about _____ grams.

Name _____ Date _____

Practice

For use with pages 90–95

Match the measures that are equivalent.

1. 72.3 km   **A.** 0.000723 km

2. 0.0723 m   **B.** 72,300 m

3. 0.723 cm   **C.** 7.23 cm

4. 723 mm   **D.** 7.23 mm

Complete the statement.

5. To convert from milliliters to _____, you divide by 1000.

6. To convert from grams to _____, you multiply by 100.

7. To convert from centimeters to _____, you divide by 100,000.

Complete the statement.

8. 2.56 g = _____ mg   9. 2614 m = _____ km

10. 0.56 L = _____ mL   11. 250,000 mg = _____ g

12. 18 m = _____ cm   13. 7.14 kg = _____ g

14. 394 cm = _____ m   15. 1.405 km = _____ m

16. 41,250 mL = _____ L

Complete the statement using <, >, or =.

17. 420 mm _____ 4.2 cm   18. 5600 mg _____ 56 g

19. 21,480 mL _____ 214.8 L   20. 6.24 m _____ 624 cm

21. 4.02 kL _____ 40,200,000 mL   22. 14 kg _____ 14,000 mg

LESSON
2.7
Continued

Name _____ Date _____

Practice
For use with pages 90–95

23. Describe and correct the error in converting 0:85 liters to milliliters.

$\times$ $0.85 \div 1000 = 0.00085$

So, 0.85 L = 0.00085 mL.

24. A bookcase is 1.98 meters tall and its shelves are 33 centimeters apart. How many shelves are in the bookcase?

25. One can of juice contains 335 milliliters of liquid. How many liters of liquid are in a 12-pack of juice?

26. The bee hummingbird, the world's smallest bird, is only 6.3 centimeters long. The ostrich, one of the world's tallest birds, can reach a height of 2.5 meters. How much longer, in centimeters, is the ostrich than the bee hummingbird?

Name _____ Date _____

Practice
For use with pages 109–114

1. Identify which of the following values is the mean of the data.

   Data: 14, 15, 24, 18, 14, 17

   A. 14   **B.** 15   **C.** 16   **D.** 17

Find the mean, median, mode(s), and range of the data.

2. 12, 25, 23, 17, 23

3. 7, 3, 9, 2, 7, 2

4. 22, 36, 9, 27, 30, 20

5. 113, 249, 312, 113, 113

6. 1, 1, 7, 3, 2, 2, 3, 5

7. 24, 3, 18, 90, 30, 13, 18

Find the value of x that makes the median the given number.

8. 2, 5, 4, 9, 7, x; median = 5

9. 32, 23, 15, 30, 12, x; median = 25

Find the value of y that makes the mean the given number.

10. 7, 8, 2, 5, y; mean = 5

11. 6, 1, 7, 4, 1, 0, y; mean = 3

Name _____ Date _____

Practice

For use with pages 109–114

The recorded high temperatures, in degrees Fahrenheit, for a city during a week in June are listed below.

77, 76, 71, 70, 69, 70, 71

12. Find the mean, median, mode(s), and range.

13. Which average(s) best represent(s) the temperatures?
Explain your reasoning.

The number of home runs per season for a baseball player for nine seasons are listed below.

7, 20, 25, 38, 40, 30, 33, 37, 49

14. Find the mean, median, mode(s), and range.

15. What happens to the mean of the home run data if the number of home runs for the first season is ignored?

16. The table shows the winning times for the men's 200-meter run in the Summer Olympics for selected years. Find the mean, median, mode(s), and range.

Year	1900	1904	1908	1912	1920	1924
Time (in seconds)	22.2	21.6	22.6	21.7	22.0	21.6

Name _____ Date _____

Practice

For use with pages 117–123

1. Describe and correct the error in creating the line graph at the right.

Year	1996	1997	1998	1999	2000	2001
Price	$1.20	$1.30	$1.10	$.40	$1.65	$1.50

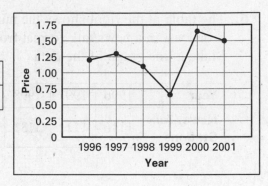

2. The table shows the heights of the tallest of each species of tree. Make a bar graph of the data.

Tallest U.S. Trees						
Species	Coast Douglas-Fir	Coast Redwood	Giant Sequoia	Sitka Spruce	Sugar Pine	Western Redcedar
Height (in feet)	281	321	275	191	232	159

3. The table shows the top five rice exporters and the amount of rice, in millions of metric tons, exported in 1998 and 1999. Make a double bar graph of the data.

Rice Exporters					
Country	Thailand	Vietnam	United States	China	India
1998	6.36	3.80	3.11	3.79	4.80
1999	6.84	4.60	2.67	2.82	2.57

4. Which country's export amount changed the most from 1998 to 1999?

Name _____ Date _____

Practice

For use with pages 117–123

5. The table at the right shows the number of radio stations that broadcast in a news/talk format from 1996 through 2000. Make a line graph of the data.

Year	1996	1997	1998	1999	2000
News/Talk Stations	1116	1111	1131	1159	1139

6. Between which years did the number of news/talk stations decrease the most? Between which years did the number of news/talk stations increase the most?

7. The table shows the price of a gallon of gasoline in Mexico from 1995 through 2000. Make a line graph of the data.

Gas Prices						
Year	1995	1996	1997	1998	1999	2000
Price (in dollars)	1.12	1.26	1.47	1.50	1.80	2.02

8. Between which years was the increase in price the greatest?

9. Make a conclusion about the data.

Name _____ Date _____

Practice
For use with pages 126–130

In Exercises 1–4, make an ordered stem-and-leaf plot of the data.

1. Quiz scores: 20, 17, 17, 15, 17, 18, 20, 9, 16, 18, 19, 20

2. Points made by a basketball player in each game: 16, 24, 28, 18, 22, 17, 24, 20, 9, 15, 20, 21

3. Plant heights in inches: 20, 18.5, 19.7, 21.2, 17.7, 17.4, 22.4, 18, 19.5, 23.4, 17, 22.6

4. Monthly precipitation in inches: 3.5, 3.1, 3.6, 3.6, 3.3, 2.6, 3.8, 4.1, 2.9, 2.8, 3.6, 3.3

The average temperatures, in degrees Fahrenheit, in Grand Junction, Colorado for each month of the year are given below.

   25, 34, 43, 52, 62, 72, 79, 76, 67, 55, 40, 29

5. Make an ordered stem-and-leaf plot of the data.

6. Make a conclusion about the data.

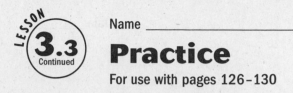

Name _____ Date _____

Practice

For use with pages 126–130

The costs, in dollars, of mailing a 2-pound package to different places outside of the United States are listed below.

   13.25, 15.50, 20.00, 20.50, 19.75, 15.50, 19.00, 19.00,
   18.75, 18.50, 22.00, 15.00, 19.00

7. Make an ordered stem-and-leaf plot of the data using the key $13.25 = 13\,|\,25$.

8. Make a conclusion about the data.

The fuel efficiency, in miles per gallon, of new passenger cars made in the United States is shown for the years the cars were produced. The standards set by the U.S. government are also given.

Year	1990	1991	1992	1993	1994	1995	1996	1997	1998	1999
Fuel Efficiency (in miles per gallon)	26.9	27.3	27.0	27.8	27.5	27.7	28.3	27.8	28.1	28.2
Standards (in miles per gallon)	27.5	27.5	27.5	27.5	27.5	27.5	27.5	27.5	27.5	27.5

9. Make an ordered stem-and-leaf plot for each set of data.

10. Make a conclusion about each stem-and-leaf plot.

11. Did the new passenger cars meet the standards most of the time? Explain your answer.

LESSON
3.4

Practice

For use with pages 133–137

Match the box-and-whisker plot with its data.

1. Data: 45, 46, 91, 72, 79, 80, 48, 52, 9, 74

2. Data: 39, 9, 81, 75, 91, 82, 51, 53, 45, 80

3. Data: 50, 47, 81, 23, 9, 91, 52, 85, 46, 67

4. Data: 79, 82, 53, 32, 63, 9, 78, 91, 65, 45

A.
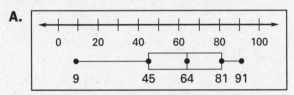

B.
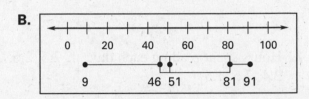

C.
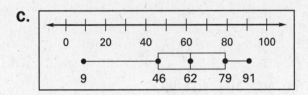

D.
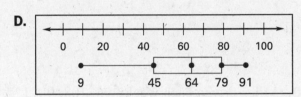

5. Describe and correct the error in making the box-and-whisker plot for the given data.

71, 69, 88, 69, 75, 46, 81, 33, 69, 65

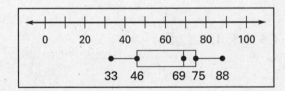

Name _____ Date _____

Practice

For use with pages 133–137

Make a box-and-whisker plot of the data.

6. Lengths of songs on a CD in seconds: 366, 421, 351, 462, 244, 495, 344, 312, 448, 287, 665

7. Hours spent reading each day: 1, 2.5, 2.6, 2.1, 1.8, 3, 3.1, 3, 2.8, 2.4, 2.5, 1.5

8. Miles driven each week: 96, 108, 90, 127, 100, 102, 103, 103, 98, 103, 107, 93

9. Weights of apples in ounces: 3.8, 4.8, 4.6, 4.2, 4.5, 3.5, 4, 4.1, 4.6, 4.7, 4.5, 3.8, 3.7

When the moon is at first quarter, the part that you can see from the Northern hemisphere is in the shape of a D. A box-and-whisker plot of the day of each month on which the moon is at first quarter in 2002 is given.

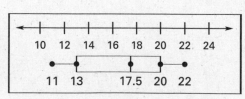

10. About what fraction of the moons at first quarter occur between the first day of the month and the thirteenth day of the month?

11. About what fraction of the moons at first quarter occur between the first day of the month and the twentieth day of the month?

Name _____ Date _____

Practice

For use with pages 138–143

Complete the frequency table using the data.

1. Total points scored in football games:
78, 26, 69, 37, 37, 73, 58, 37, 69,
48, 82, 27, 36, 37, 37, 73, 37, 54,
38, 28, 29

Interval	Tally	Frequency
26–40		
55–68		
69–82		

2. Minimum heights for amusement park rides:
48, 42, 48, 36, 48, 46, 42, 48, 48, 46,
48, 48, 48, 46, 48, 36, 48, 48, 46,
46, 46, 48, 46, 36, 39, 46

Interval	Tally	Frequency
40–43		
44–47		

3. The total numbers of songs on different CDs are given below.
Describe and correct the error(s) in the frequency table.

12, 8, 11, 12, 11, 8, 5, 8, 10, 11, 14, 11, 9, 8, 6, 13,
14, 11, 14, 12, 10, 10, 10, 18, 20, 6

Interval	Tally	Frequency
5–9	ⅢⅠ Ⅲ	8
9–13	ⅢⅠ ⅢⅠ ⅢⅠ	14
13–17	ⅢⅠ	4
17–20	Ⅱ	2

4. Which intervals can be used to make a frequency table of the data?

32, 38, 49, 25, 31, 31, 56, 24, 28, 58, 25, 31, 40, 52, 61, 52, 34, 27, 69, 63, 45

A. 0–10, 11–20, 21–30, 31–40, 41–50, 51–60, 61–70

B. 25–35, 35–45, 45–55, 55–65, 65–75

C. 20–30, 31–40, 41–50, 51–60, 61–70

D. 21–30, 31–40, 41–50, 51–60, 61–70

Name _____ Date _____

Practice

For use with pages 138–143

The days of the month in January and February of 2003 on which the New York Philharmonic was scheduled to perform are given below.

> **2, 3, 7, 9, 11, 12, 14, 16, 17, 18, 22, 23, 24, 25, 30, 31, 1, 14, 19, 20, 21, 22, 26, 27, 28**

5. Make a histogram of the data.

6. Make a conclusion about the data.

The magnitudes, or intensities, of recorded major earthquakes from 1998 through 2001 are listed below.

> **6.1, 6.6, 6.9, 6.3, 7.1, 6.4, 7.4, 5.8, 7.6, 4.6, 7.5, 5.9, 7.5, 5.3, 8.0, 5.1, 4.9, 5.8, 7.5, 6.8, 7.7, 7.7, 6.6, 5.4, 6.8, 8.4**

7. Make a histogram of the data.

Practice

For use with pages 144–149

Tell which of the given types of data displays would be appropriate for the set of data. Then make the data display.

1. A bar graph or a histogram

Average Earnings in 1999 for Women with a Bachelor's Degree or Higher					
Age	18–24	25–34	35–44	45–54	55–64
Earnings	$19,007	$34,195	$40,012	$41,096	$37,801

2. A stem-and-leaf plot or a box-and-whisker plot

Prices for One Share of Restaurant Stock						
$64.06	$59.50	$37.07	$26.36	$12.01	$33.66	$27.20
$3.45	$6.61	$32.80	$10.74	$41.16	$22.01	$29.82

3. The table below shows the cost of mailing a three-ounce package to other areas of the world. Choose an appropriate data display for the data. Explain your choice.

Country	Canada	Mexico	Europe	Australia, Japan, New Zealand	Other countries
Cost	$1.10	$1.25	$2.40	$2.60	$2.30

Name _____ Date _____

Practice

For use with pages 144–149

4. Explain why the line graph for the population of Omaha, Nebraska could be misleading. Create a line graph for the data that is not misleading.

Year	Population
1950	251,117
1960	301,598
1970	347,000
1980	314,000
1990	335,795
2000	390,007

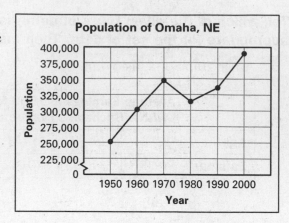

The graph shows the amounts of corn produced in various countries in 2000.

5. Which country had three times the production of the Czech Republic?

6. Which country had half the production of the Czech Republic?

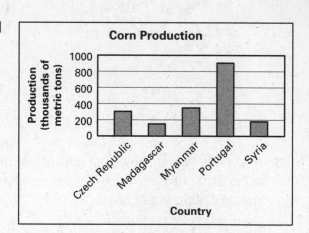

LESSON
4.1

Name _____ Date _____

Practice

For use with pages 165–169

Write all the factors of the number.

1. 29

2. 63

3. 70

4. 34

5. 120

6. 66

Tell whether the number is *prime* or *composite*. Explain your reasoning.

7. 98

8. 41

9. 57

10. 59

11. 73

12. 25

13. Describe and correct the error in writing the prime factorization of 56.

Complete the factor tree.

14.

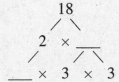

15.

16.

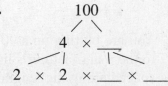

McDougal Littell Math, Course 2
Chapter 4   Practice Workbook

41

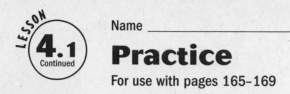
Use a factor tree to write the prime factorization of the number.

17. 72

18. 125

19. 44

20. 95

21. 156

22. 77

23. You are planning to put a tile border along a 126-inch-wide wall in your kitchen. You want to use only whole tiles. List all the possible whole number tile widths you could use. If the tiles are only sold in whole number widths of 6 inches or less, what size tiles could you use?

24. You are putting up a 90-foot-long fence in your backyard. According to the manufacturer's instructions, the fence posts should be equally spaced along the length of the yard. List all the possible spacing options if the amount of space between the posts is a whole number of feet. If the posts should be spaced between 8 feet and 14 feet apart, how far apart should your posts be?

Name _____ Date _____

Practice

For use with pages 170–174

Find the greatest common factor of the numbers by listing factors.

1. 42, 90   **2.** 34, 68   **3.** 56, 150

4. 28, 45   **5.** 60, 350   **6.** 40, 68

Find the greatest common factor of the numbers using prime factorization. Then tell whether the numbers are relatively prime.

7. 30, 135   **8.** 45, 56   **9.** 99, 165

10. 132, 198   **11.** 20, 88, 165   **12.** 168, 180, 450

13. Which numbers are relatively prime?

    A. 180, 231   **B.** 120, 147   **C.** 75, 112   **D.** 75, 360

14. Describe and correct the error in finding the greatest common factor of 60 and 126.

    Factors of 60: 1, 2, 3, 4, 5, 6, 10, 12, 15, 20, 30, 60
    Factors of 126: 1, 2, 3, 6, 7, 9, 14, 18, 21, 42, 63, 126

The greatest common factor of 60 and 126 is $2 \times 3 \times 6 = 36$.

Name _____ Date _____

Practice

For use with pages 170–174

15. The greatest common factor of two numbers is 5. What could the two numbers be?

16. You made 63 wheat dinner rolls, 45 rye dinner rolls, and 54 sourdough dinner rolls for a family picnic. You want to make up plates of rolls to set on the picnic tables. If each plate is to contain the same amount of each type of roll, and there are no leftover rolls, what is the greatest number of plates that can be made? How many wheat dinner rolls, rye dinner rolls, and sourdough dinner rolls are on each plate?

17. A college class with 30 sophomores, 18 juniors, and 12 seniors is divided into project groups where each group has the same number of sophomores, juniors, and seniors. What is the greatest number of groups that can be formed? How many sophomores, juniors, and seniors are in each project group?

18. A piece of paper is 280 millimeters long and 200 millimeters wide. You want to draw a grid on the paper so that there is a whole number of squares on the paper. What are the possible sizes of the squares? What is the largest possible square?

Name _____ Date _____

Practice

For use with pages 176–180

Match the equivalent fractions.

1. $\dfrac{8}{12}$ A. $\dfrac{24}{30}$

2. $\dfrac{4}{5}$ B. $\dfrac{24}{54}$

3. $\dfrac{6}{8}$ C. $\dfrac{10}{15}$

4. $\dfrac{4}{9}$ D. $\dfrac{42}{56}$

Write two fractions that are equivalent to the given fraction.

5. $\dfrac{28}{44}$ 6. $\dfrac{42}{60}$ 7. $\dfrac{45}{90}$

Write the fraction in simplest form.

8. $\dfrac{22}{66}$ 9. $\dfrac{42}{105}$ 10. $\dfrac{78}{90}$

11. $\dfrac{24}{48}$ 12. $\dfrac{54}{60}$ 13. $\dfrac{51}{68}$

Name _____ Date _____

Practice

For use with pages 176–180

Write the fractions in simplest form. Tell whether they are equivalent.

14. $\frac{4}{14}, \frac{10}{35}$

15. $\frac{60}{96}, \frac{35}{56}$

16. $\frac{25}{40}, \frac{60}{84}$

17. $\frac{40}{75}, \frac{36}{60}$

18. $\frac{36}{39}, \frac{72}{78}$

19. $\frac{60}{132}, \frac{48}{88}$

20. You have completed 32 problems of history homework and you have 16 problems left. What fraction of the problems have you completed? Write the fraction in simplest form.

21. You are on a road trip and make a rest stop after being on the road for 85 miles. You have another 55 miles to go until you reach your destination. What fraction of the trip have you completed? Write the fraction in simplest form.

22. A bag of 24 balloons contains 16 yellow balloons. A larger bag of 50 balloons contains 33 yellow balloons. For each bag of balloons, write a fraction in simplest form comparing the number of yellow balloons to the total number of balloons. Are the fractions equivalent?

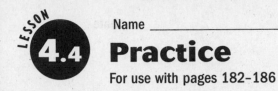

Name _____ Date _____

Practice

For use with pages 182–186

Find the LCM of the numbers by listing multiples.

1. 9, 12

2. 5, 14

3. 12, 16

4. 15, 20

5. 4, 9, 12

6. 8, 9, 24

Find the LCM of the numbers using prime factorization.

7. 42, 126

8. 75, 105

9. 54, 210

10. 30, 50

11. 72, 108

12. 8, 30, 45

Find the GCF and the LCM of the numbers using prime factorization.

13. 18, 20

14. 60, 72

15. 56, 84

16. 12, 27

17. 16, 63, 75

18. 36, 60, 135

Name _____ Date _____

Practice

For use with pages 182–186

19. Describe and correct the error in finding the least common multiple of 8 and 60.

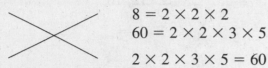

$8 = 2 \times 2 \times 2$
$60 = 2 \times 2 \times 3 \times 5$
$2 \times 2 \times 3 \times 5 = 60$

So, the LCM of 8 and 60 is 60.

20. Which two number pairs have the same LCM?

A. 3, 16   **B.** 4, 14   **C.** 6, 8   **D.** 8, 12

Find the LCM of the denominators of the fractions.

21. $\dfrac{1}{3}, \dfrac{1}{2}$ **22.** $\dfrac{2}{5}, \dfrac{1}{8}$ **23.** $\dfrac{1}{2}, \dfrac{5}{6}$

24. During the summer, you mow lawns for extra money. One customer pays you to mow the lawn every 6 days and another customer pays you to mow the lawn every 9 days. If you mow both lawns today, in how many days will you mow both lawns again on the same day? If today is Monday, on what day of the week will you mow both lawns again on the same day?

25. At an animal rehabilitation center, the baby rabbits need to be fed every 8 hours and the baby squirrels need to be fed every 6 hours. If the rabbits and squirrels are both fed at 9:30 A.M., when will they be fed again at the same time?

Name _____ Date _____

Practice
For use with pages 189–193

Complete the statement using <, >, or =.

1. $\dfrac{3}{4}$ _____ $\dfrac{9}{16}$

2. $\dfrac{3}{5}$ _____ $\dfrac{7}{8}$

3. $\dfrac{2}{9}$ _____ $\dfrac{7}{15}$

4. $\dfrac{7}{12}$ _____ $\dfrac{5}{18}$

5. $\dfrac{5}{8}$ _____ $\dfrac{15}{24}$

6. $\dfrac{12}{35}$ _____ $\dfrac{2}{5}$

7. Which fraction is between $\dfrac{3}{5}$ and $\dfrac{3}{4}$?

A. $\dfrac{11}{20}$ **B.** $\dfrac{12}{15}$ **C.** $\dfrac{34}{40}$ **D.** $\dfrac{8}{11}$

Order the fractions from least to greatest.

8. $\dfrac{3}{4}, \dfrac{5}{48}, \dfrac{3}{8}, \dfrac{5}{6}$

9. $\dfrac{4}{5}, \dfrac{5}{8}, \dfrac{11}{20}, \dfrac{3}{10}$

10. $\dfrac{8}{9}, \dfrac{2}{3}, \dfrac{10}{27}, \dfrac{15}{18}$

11. $\dfrac{3}{4}, \dfrac{11}{24}, \dfrac{13}{18}, \dfrac{8}{9}$

12. $\dfrac{4}{15}, \dfrac{7}{12}, \dfrac{4}{5}, \dfrac{23}{30}$

13. $\dfrac{11}{15}, \dfrac{7}{18}, \dfrac{3}{5}, \dfrac{5}{9}$

Name _____ Date _____

Practice

For use with pages 189–193

Use approximation to tell which fraction is greater.

14. $\dfrac{5}{12}, \dfrac{17}{30}$

15. $\dfrac{5}{24}, \dfrac{9}{35}$

16. $\dfrac{13}{30}, \dfrac{25}{41}$

17. $\dfrac{9}{28}, \dfrac{11}{54}$

18. $\dfrac{31}{130}, \dfrac{22}{75}$

19. $\dfrac{31}{55}, \dfrac{52}{110}$

20. In 2001, 32 out of 80 members of New Jersey's House of Representatives were Democrats and 25 out of 60 members of Oregon's House of Representatives were Democrats. For each state, write a fraction for the number of Democrats in the House to the total number of House members. Which state had a greater fraction of Democrats in its House of Representatives?

21. In the recently completed season, a baseball player hit the ball 70 times out of the 254 times he was at bat. In the previous season, the player hit the ball 50 times out of the 210 times he was at bat. For each season, write a fraction for the number of hits to the total number of times at bat. In which season was the ball hit a greater fraction of the time?

Name _____ Date _____

Practice

For use with pages 194–198

Write the mixed number as an improper fraction.

1. $4\frac{1}{4}$

2. $3\frac{2}{3}$

3. $2\frac{6}{7}$

4. $5\frac{4}{9}$

5. $6\frac{3}{10}$

6. $8\frac{2}{15}$

Write the improper fraction as a mixed number.

7. $\frac{11}{2}$

8. $\frac{15}{4}$

9. $\frac{53}{10}$

10. $\frac{23}{3}$

11. $\frac{51}{11}$

12. $\frac{53}{16}$

13. Describe and correct the error in writing $5\frac{4}{9}$ as an improper fraction.

$$5\frac{4}{9} = \frac{5 \times 4 + 9}{9} = \frac{29}{9}$$

14. Which number is between $\frac{34}{9}$ and $3\frac{8}{9}$?

A. $\frac{37}{9}$

B. $3\frac{5}{6}$

C. $3\frac{5}{9}$

D. $\frac{31}{9}$

Practice

For use with pages 194–198

Order the numbers from least to greatest.

15. $2\frac{2}{5}, \frac{11}{5}, 2\frac{3}{10}, \frac{31}{10}$

16. $4\frac{1}{2}, \frac{19}{4}, \frac{37}{8}, 4\frac{3}{16}$

17. $\frac{23}{3}, 7\frac{4}{9}, \frac{55}{9}, 7\frac{5}{18}$

18. $4\frac{11}{24}, 5\frac{1}{4}, \frac{31}{6}, \frac{57}{12}$

19. $1\frac{3}{4}, 2\frac{2}{5}, \frac{21}{10}, \frac{29}{20}$

20. $9\frac{1}{6}, 10\frac{1}{4}, \frac{61}{6}, \frac{83}{9}$

21. A recipe for whole-wheat bread calls for $2\frac{1}{4}$ cups of flour. If you only have a one-fourth cup measure, how many one-fourth cups of flour do you need?

22. The top four discus throws at a track meet are $97\frac{1}{8}$ feet, $97\frac{3}{5}$ feet, $97\frac{1}{4}$ feet, and $97\frac{2}{9}$ feet. Order the numbers from least to greatest. What is the distance of the longest throw?

Practice

For use with pages 199–204

Match the number with its point on the number line.

1. $2\frac{7}{8}$

2. 2.65

3. $2.\overline{4}$

4. $\frac{61}{20}$

```
          A   B   C   D
←+—+—+—+—•—+—•—+—•—+—•—+—+—→
 2.0 2.2 2.4 2.6 2.8 3.0 3.2
```

Write the fraction or mixed number as a decimal.
Then tell whether the decimal is a *terminating decimal*
or a *repeating decimal*.

5. $\frac{2}{5}$

6. $\frac{8}{3}$

7. $5\frac{3}{4}$

8. $4\frac{2}{9}$

9. $\frac{16}{5}$

10. $9\frac{11}{20}$

Rewrite the repeating decimal using bar notation.

11. $0.4444\ldots$

12. $2.161616\ldots$

13. $3.67777\ldots$

Name _____ Date _____

Practice
For use with pages 199–204

Write the decimal as a fraction or mixed number.

14. 0.6

15. 0.18

16. 3.25

17. 1.375

18. 0.125

19. 6.34

Order the numbers from least to greatest.

20. $\frac{2}{5}$, 0.34, $\frac{7}{3}$, 0.3, 0.$\overline{3}$

21. $\frac{23}{4}$, 5.65, $5\frac{4}{5}$, 5.$\overline{6}$

22. $\frac{23}{20}$, $1\frac{1}{5}$, 1.01, 1.$\overline{15}$

23. At 31.04 miles, the English Channel Tunnel is one of the world's longest railway tunnels. Write the length as an improper fraction and as a mixed number.

24. In 1991, Mike Powell set the men's long jump world record with a jump of $29\frac{3}{8}$ feet. Write the distance as an improper fraction and as a decimal.

25. In the United States, the five Great Lakes cover an area of 94,710 square miles. The smallest of the Great Lakes, Lake Ontario, covers an area of 7540 square miles. Write a fraction in simplest form that compares the area of Lake Ontario to the total area of all the Great Lakes. Then write the fraction as a decimal to the nearest hundredth.

Name _____ Date _____

Practice

For use with pages 219–224

Find the sum or difference. Write the answer in simplest form.

1. $\dfrac{3}{10} + \dfrac{4}{10}$

2. $\dfrac{5}{8} - \dfrac{3}{8}$

3. $\dfrac{6}{11} + \dfrac{2}{11}$

4. $\dfrac{4}{5} - \dfrac{1}{5}$

5. $\dfrac{5}{16} - \dfrac{1}{16}$

6. $\dfrac{17}{30} - \dfrac{11}{30}$

7. $\dfrac{3}{4} + \dfrac{5}{8}$

8. $\dfrac{7}{10} - \dfrac{1}{2}$

9. $\dfrac{2}{3} + \dfrac{5}{12}$

10. $\dfrac{1}{2} + \dfrac{3}{5}$

11. $\dfrac{6}{7} - \dfrac{1}{4}$

12. $\dfrac{4}{15} + \dfrac{5}{12}$

13. Describe and correct the error in finding the sum $\frac{3}{5} + \frac{4}{9}$.

$$\frac{3}{5} + \frac{4}{9} = \frac{15}{45} + \frac{36}{45} = \frac{51}{45} = 1\frac{2}{15}$$

Evaluate the expression when $x = \frac{1}{3}$ and $y = \frac{2}{5}$.

14. $x + \dfrac{1}{7}$

15. $\dfrac{5}{6} - y$

16. $x + y$

Name _____ Date _____

Practice

For use with pages 219–224

Use mental math to solve the equation.

17. $\dfrac{7}{8} = \dfrac{5}{8} + x$

18. $x + \dfrac{5}{11} = \dfrac{9}{11}$

19. $\dfrac{5}{6} - x = \dfrac{2}{6}$

Complete the statement using <, >, or =.

20. $\dfrac{3}{5} + \dfrac{4}{7}$ _____ 1

21. $\dfrac{3}{8} + \dfrac{7}{18}$ _____ 1

22. $\dfrac{25}{51} + \dfrac{10}{17}$ _____ 1

23. Carriage bolts are sold in a variety of lengths. Two carriage bolt lengths are $\dfrac{3}{8}$ inch and $\dfrac{1}{2}$ inch. How much longer is the $\dfrac{1}{2}$-inch bolt than the $\dfrac{3}{8}$-inch bolt?

24. You are estimating the total distance of a road trip by measuring the distance on a map. On the map, the legs of the trip measure $\dfrac{11}{16}$ inch, $\dfrac{5}{8}$ inch, and $\dfrac{1}{4}$ inch, respectively. What is the total distance of the trip on the map?

Name _____ Date _____

Practice

For use with pages 226–230

Find the sum or difference. Write the answer in simplest form.

1. $3\frac{2}{7} + 4\frac{5}{7}$

2. $5\frac{7}{12} - 3\frac{5}{12}$

3. $2\frac{3}{8} + 1\frac{7}{8}$

4. $8\frac{14}{15} - 5\frac{8}{15}$

5. $1\frac{2}{5} + 6\frac{8}{15}$

6. $5\frac{7}{9} - 3\frac{5}{18}$

7. $4\frac{5}{6} + 7\frac{7}{24}$

8. $10\frac{17}{21} - 4\frac{2}{3}$

9. $5\frac{3}{7} + 4\frac{1}{2}$

10. $8\frac{1}{4} - 3\frac{1}{3}$

11. $3\frac{5}{12} + 7\frac{2}{15}$

12. $5\frac{1}{9} - 2\frac{5}{6}$

13. Describe and correct the error in finding the difference $8\frac{1}{6} - 4\frac{2}{3}$.

$$8\frac{1}{6} - 4\frac{2}{3} = 8\frac{1}{6} - 4\frac{4}{6} = 7\frac{9}{6} - 4\frac{4}{6} = 3\frac{5}{6}$$

Evaluate the expression when $x = 4\frac{3}{8}$ and $y = 7\frac{5}{6}$.

14. $5\frac{2}{3} + x$

15. $y - 4\frac{2}{3}$

16. $x + y$

Name _____ Date _____

Practice

For use with pages 226–230

Complete the statement using <, >, or =.

17. $8\frac{2}{3} - 7\frac{1}{4}$ ____ 1

18. $4\frac{1}{6} + 5\frac{3}{8}$ ____ 10

19. $7\frac{1}{4} + 3\frac{3}{7}$ ____ 11

Evaluate the expression. Write the answer in simplest form.

20. $3\frac{1}{2} + 6\frac{2}{3} + 4\frac{7}{12}$ **21.** $8\frac{9}{16} - 3\frac{1}{4} + 5\frac{3}{8}$ **22.** $12\frac{5}{24} - 8\frac{3}{4} + 7\frac{1}{8}$

23. A rye bread recipe calls for $1\frac{7}{8}$ cups bread flour and $1\frac{1}{2}$ cups rye flour. How many cups of flour do you need altogether?

24. The largest species of praying mantis grows to be about 6 inches long. The smallest species of praying mantis grows to be $\frac{2}{5}$ inches long. How much longer is the largest species than the smallest species?

Name _____ Date _____

Practice
For use with pages 232–236

Find the product. Write the answer in simplest form.

1. $\dfrac{1}{8} \times \dfrac{3}{7}$

2. $\dfrac{4}{5} \times \dfrac{10}{11}$

3. $\dfrac{6}{7} \times \dfrac{15}{16}$

4. $\dfrac{7}{10} \times \dfrac{25}{28}$

5. $12 \times \dfrac{3}{4}$

6. $\dfrac{5}{6} \times 24$

7. $2\dfrac{2}{3} \times 1\dfrac{4}{5}$

8. $8\dfrac{1}{2} \times 1\dfrac{7}{9}$

9. $5\dfrac{3}{4} \times 10\dfrac{2}{3}$

10. Find the area of the rectangle.

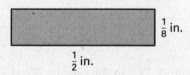

$\frac{1}{8}$ in.

$\frac{1}{2}$ in.

11. Which two products have the same value?

A. $1\dfrac{1}{3} \times \dfrac{2}{5}$ **B.** $1\dfrac{2}{3} \times \dfrac{3}{5}$ **C.** $1\dfrac{1}{4} \times 1\dfrac{1}{2}$ **D.** $\dfrac{4}{5} \times \dfrac{2}{3}$

Name _____ Date _____

Practice

For use with pages 232–236

Evaluate the expression when $x = 4$ and $y = 10$.

12. $\frac{3}{4}x$

13. $\frac{5}{7} \cdot \frac{1}{y}$

14. $\frac{18}{25} \cdot \frac{3}{x}$

15. Choose the product that best estimates $5\frac{2}{3} \times 4\frac{1}{5}$.

    A. 5×4 **B.** 6×4 **C.** 6×5 **D.** 5×5

Use mental math to solve the equation.

16. $\frac{a}{4} \cdot 3 = \frac{3}{4}$

17. $\frac{2}{5} \cdot b = \frac{12}{5}$

18. $8 \cdot \frac{6}{c} = \frac{48}{13}$

19. A deer mouse is $7\frac{1}{4}$ inches long, including its tail. If the tail is one-half its total body length, how long is the tail?

20. A mirror is $13\frac{1}{2}$ inches wide and $21\frac{1}{4}$ inches long. What is the area of the mirror?

Name _____ Date _____

Practice

For use with pages 237–241

Write the reciprocal of the number.

1. $\frac{1}{5}$ **2.** 2 **3.** $1\frac{4}{5}$ **4.** $3\frac{6}{11}$

Find the quotient. Then check your answer.

5. $\frac{2}{9} \div \frac{1}{3}$ **6.** $\frac{3}{4} \div \frac{5}{8}$ **7.** $\frac{4}{9} \div \frac{9}{20}$

8. $\frac{2}{3} \div \frac{5}{18}$ **9.** $\frac{9}{14} \div 7$ **10.** $9 \div 4\frac{2}{3}$

11. $6\frac{3}{4} \div 5\frac{1}{2}$ **12.** $3\frac{2}{5} \div 8$ **13.** $4\frac{1}{6} \div 3\frac{2}{5}$

14. Describe and correct the error in finding the quotient $\frac{4}{5} \div 3\frac{2}{3}$.

$$\frac{4}{5} \div 3\frac{2}{3} = \frac{4}{5} \div \frac{11}{3} = \frac{5}{4} \times \frac{11}{3} = 4\frac{7}{12}$$

Name _____ Date _____

Practice
For use with pages 237–241

Evaluate the expression when $x = \frac{3}{5}$ and $y = 8$.

15. $x \div y$

16. $y \div x$

17. $1\frac{1}{3} \div x$

Complete the statement using $<$, $>$, or $=$.

18. $\frac{1}{2} \div \frac{2}{5}$ _____ 1

19. $\frac{7}{8} \div \frac{1}{9}$ _____ 1

20. $1\frac{2}{5} \div 2\frac{1}{4}$ _____ 1

Use mental math to solve the equation.

21. $\frac{5}{a} \div 3 = \frac{5}{3}$

22. $\frac{b}{4} \div \frac{1}{8} = 6$

23. $\frac{2}{3} \div c = \frac{4}{3}$

24. You are cutting fabric for placemats that are to be $14\frac{1}{4}$ inches wide. If you have a piece of fabric that is 114 inches long, how many placemats can you cut from the fabric?

25. The largest and smallest sea urchins on record measured about $1\frac{1}{4}$ feet and $\frac{1}{50}$ foot long, respectively. How many times larger is the largest sea urchin?

Name _____ Date _____

Practice

For use with pages 245–249

Estimate the length of the object. Then measure the object using a ruler.

1. your hand

2. a spoon

3. a textbook

4. Determine the weight of the fruit by reading the scale.

5. Determine how much liquid is in the measuring cup.

Complete the statement using the appropriate customary unit.

6. A hockey puck weighs 6 _____.

7. A sauce pan holds $\frac{1}{2}$ _____.

8. A minivan is 201 _____ long.

9. A horse weighs 1110 _____.

10. An oil drum holds 55 _____.

11. A toothpick is $2\frac{1}{4}$ _____ long.

Name _____ Date _____

Practice

For use with pages 245–249

Choose the letter of the most reasonable measurement.

12. The length of a golf club is ____.

    A. 3 yd

    B. 5 in.

    C. 7 ft

    D. $40\frac{1}{2}$ in.

13. The weight of a hamster is ____.

    A. 75 oz

    B. $\frac{1}{3}$ lb

    C. 2 oz

    D. $4\frac{3}{4}$ lb

14. The capacity of a garbage can is ____.

    A. 13 gal

    B. 12 qt

    C. 64 fl oz

    D. 2 gal

Complete the statement using 3, 30, or 300.

15. A jug of laundry detergent holds ____ fluid ounces.

16. A dog water dish holds ____ cups.

Name _____ Date _____

Practice

For use with pages 250–255

Complete the statement.

1. $7\frac{1}{3}$ yd = _____ ft

2. $5\frac{1}{2}$ T = _____ lb

3. $9\frac{3}{4}$ qt = _____ pt

4. 15,840 ft = _____ mi

5. 20 oz = _____ lb

6. $10\frac{2}{3}$ c = _____ pt

7. 78 in. = _____ yd

8. 3 T = _____ oz

9. 5 c = _____ fl oz

Find the sum or difference.

10.   7 yd 4 ft
    + 9 yd 2 ft

11.   5 lb 9 oz
    + 17 lb 9 oz

12.   8 c 3 fl oz
    − 3 c 6 fl oz

Complete the statement using <, >, or =.

13. $5\frac{2}{3}$ ft _____ 65 in.

14. $1\frac{3}{4}$ lb _____ 25 oz

15. $3\frac{1}{2}$ c _____ 28 fl oz

16. 4000 ft _____ $\frac{3}{4}$ mi

17. $5\frac{3}{5}$ lb _____ 92 oz

18. $\frac{3}{4}$ gal _____ 6 pt

19. Describe and correct the error in converting $5\frac{1}{3}$ cups to quarts.

$$5\frac{1}{3} \text{ c} = \frac{16 \cancel{c}}{3} \times \frac{2 \text{ pt}}{1 \cancel{c}} \times \frac{1 \text{ qt}}{2 \cancel{pt}} = \frac{16}{3} \text{ qt} = 5\frac{1}{3} \text{ qt}$$

Name _____ Date _____

Practice

For use with pages 250–255

Order the measurements from least to greatest.

20. $5\frac{1}{2}$ ft, $1\frac{2}{3}$ yd, 69 in., 5 ft 3 in.

21. $7\frac{1}{3}$ c, 58 fl oz, $3\frac{1}{4}$ pt, 60 fl oz

22. A recipe for caesar dressing calls for $\frac{3}{4}$ cups of olive oil. Convert the amount of olive oil to fluid ounces.

23. The names of the three longest suspension bridges in the United States and their lengths are shown below. Determine which bridge is the longest.

Bridge	Golden Gate	Mackinac Straits	Verrazano-Narrows
Length	1400 yds	3800 ft	51,120 in.

Name _____ Date _____

Practice
For use with pages 269–273

Write the integer that represents the situation. Then write the opposite of that integer.

1. A $52 account withdrawal

2. Seventeen degrees below zero

Draw a number line and graph the integer. Then give a real-life situation that the integer could represent.

3. -6

4. 2

5. the opposite of 4

Complete the statement using < or >.

6. 27 ____ -72

7. -8 ____ -15

8. 62 ____ 59

9. -12 ____ 6

10. 35 ____ -35

11. -8 ____ 2

Name two integer values of the variable that make the statement true.

12. $0 < x$

13. $a < 32$

14. $-18 > y$

Name _____ Date _____

Practice

For use with pages 269–273

Order the integers from least to greatest.

15. 16, −5, 8, −23, 51, 0

16. −30, 20, 9, −12, 0, −10

17. 89, −44, 15, −3, 9, −48

18. −130, 215, −501, 125, −42, 18

Tell whether the statement is *true* or *false*. Explain your reasoning.

19. $-8 < 7$

20. $-14 > -18$

21. $5 > -2$

22. $-5 > -1$

23. $0 > -12$

24. $-24 < -27$

25. The lowest temperature recorded in Indiana was 36 degrees below zero. The lowest temperature recorded in Arkansas was 29 degrees below zero. Which temperature was lower?

26. The table lists five countries and the number of hours each country's time is ahead of or behind Eastern Standard Time (EST). Use a number line to order the number of hours from least to greatest. Let positive integers represent the number of hours ahead of EST and let negative integers represent the number of hours behind EST.

Country or Territory	Hours from EST
American Samoa	6 hours behind
Costa Rica	1 hour behind
Cuba	0 hours ahead
French Polynesia	5 hours behind
Germany	6 hours ahead

Name _____ Date _____

Practice

For use with pages 277–282

Write the addition expression modeled on the number line. Then find the sum.

1.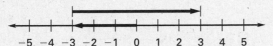

2.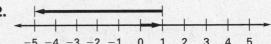

Find the absolute value of the number.

3. 25   **4.** -13 **5.** 0

Find the sum.

6. $14 + (-8)$ **7.** $-35 + 24$ **8.** $-5 + (-12)$

9. $-19 + 23$ **10.** $18 + (-31)$ **11.** $-8 + (-15)$

12. $13 + (-13)$ **13.** $-3 + 17 + (-4)$ **14.** $5 + (-11) + 14$

Complete the statement using <, >, or =.

15. $|-8|$ ____ 5   **16.** 0 ____ $|-12|$ **17.** $|-6|$ ____ $|6|$

18. -7 ____ $|3|$ **19.** $|-4|$ ____ $|-9|$ **20.** 13 ____ $-13|$

Name _____ Date _____

Practice

For use with pages 277–282

Evaluate the expression when $a = 8$ and $b = -5$.

21. $-17 + a$ **22.** $b + (-4)$ **23.** $3 + a + b$

24. Which addition expression has a sum of 11?

     A. $27 + (-15)$ **B.** $-8 + (-3)$ **C.** $-14 + 25$ **D.** $20 + (-31)$

25. In January, the normal high temperature in Bismark, North Dakota, is 22 degrees warmer than its normal low temperature. If Bismark's normal low temperature is $-2°F$ in January, what is its normal high temperature?

26. At the beginning of the week, you have $42 in your savings account. During the week, you deposit $25 and withdraw $36. How much money is in your account at the end of the week?

27. The lowest point in Europe is the Caspian Sea at an elevation of 92 feet below sea level. The highest point in Europe is Mount Elbrus, which is 18,602 feet above the Caspian Sea. What is the elevation of Mount Elbrus?

Name _____ Date _____

Practice

For use with pages 285–289

Find the difference.

1. $-16 - 7$

2. $14 - (-17)$

3. $11 - 28$

4. $30 - 12$

5. $5 - (-5)$

6. $-4 - (-34)$

7. $-63 - (-9)$

8. $-44 - 35$

9. $52 - (-79)$

Evaluate the expression when $a = 5$ and $b = -14$.

10. $b - a$

11. $a - b$

12. $12 - b + a$

Use mental math to solve the equation.

13. $6 - a = 11$

14. $-3 - x = -14$

15. $-12 - c = 24$

Evaluate the expression.

16. $-3 - (-4) + 5$

17. $4 - 8 - (-16)$

18. $-17 + 15 - (-12)$

Name _____ Date _____

Practice

For use with pages 285–289

Tell whether the statement is *true* or *false*.

19. The difference of a positive integer and a negative integer is always positive.

20. The difference of a negative integer and a negative integer is always negative.

21. The difference of a negative integer and a positive integer is sometimes positive.

22. The highest point in California is Mount Whitney at 14,494 feet above sea level. The lowest point in California is Death Valley at 282 feet below sea level. What is the difference in the elevations?

23. A temperature expressed using Kelvin (K) units can be converted to degrees Celsius (°C) by subtracting 273. Convert the boiling points of the gases given in the table from Kelvin to degrees Celsius.

Gas	Boiling Point
Argon	87 K
Helium	4 K
Krypton	120 K
Neon	27 K

24. The temperature at 6 P.M. was 8°F. Three hours later the temperature was −11°F. What was the change in temperature?

Name _____ Date _____

Practice

For use with pages 291–295

Find the product.

1. 4(15)

2. 8(−6)

3. −11(9)

4. −24(−3)

5. −14(5)

6. 25(−30)

7. −17(0)

8. −3(2)(5)

9. −2(−5)(4)

10. 150(−4)

11. −200(−75)

12. −8(0)(7)

Complete the statement using <, >, or =.

13. 17(−3) _____ 25(−2)

14. −18(−2) _____ 7(5)

15. −24(2) _____ 6(−8)

Evaluate the expression.

16. −3(6) + 4

17. 2(−8) − 3

18. −5(−4) + 8

Name _____ Date _____

Practice

For use with pages 291–295

Evaluate the expression when $a = -4$, $b = -3$, and $c = -9$.

19. ab **20.** b^3 **21.** $5ac$

22. $-7ab$ **23.** $0a^2$ **24.** $8c$

Solve the equation using mental math.

25. $-4x = 32$ **26.** $3a = -36$ **27.** $-2b = -28$

28. A beluga whale is diving downward at a speed of 2 meters per second. What integer represents the whale's change in position after 45 seconds?

29. The record low temperature in Louisiana is $-16°F$. The record low temperature in Maine is three times lower than the record low in Louisiana. What is the record low temperature in Maine?

30. A sump pump can be used to pump large amounts of water out of basements that have been flooded. One sump pump model removes water from a basement at a rate of 45 gallons per minute. Write and simplify an expression to represent the change in the amount of water in the basement after 5 minutes.

Name _____ Date _____

Practice

For use with pages 296–300

Find the quotient.

1. $-66 \div 11$

2. $72 \div (-3)$

3. $-96 \div (-12)$

4. $80 \div (-20)$

5. $-125 \div (-5)$

6. $-124 \div 31$

7. $0 \div (-23)$

8. $-325 \div 13$

9. $-147 \div (-7)$

Find the mean of the integers.

10. $-5, 0, 2, 3$

11. $-8, -6, 5, 5$

12. $-4, -3, 1, 3, 8$

13. $-6, -5, 5, 7, 9$

14. $9, -12, 19, -9$

15. $5, 12, -12, -5, 0$

Convert the temperature from degrees Fahrenheit to degrees Celsius or from degrees Celsius to degrees Fahrenheit.
[Use $F = \frac{9}{5}C + 32$ and $C = \frac{5}{9}(F - 32)$.]

16. $-45°C$

17. $115°C$

18. $59°F$

Name _____ Date _____

Practice

For use with pages 296–300

Evaluate the expression when *m* = 25 and *n* = −6.

19. $m \div (-5)$ **20.** $-54 \div n$ **21.** $-225 \div m$

22. $0 \div n$ **23.** $n \div 3$ **24.** $78 \div n$

Complete the statement using <, >, or =.

25. $15 \div (-3)$ ____ $15 \div 3$ **26.** $76 \div (-19)$ ____ $-76 \div 19$

27. $24 \div 8$ ____ $-24 \div 8$ **28.** $0 \div 5$ ____ $0 \div 9$

29. $42 \div (-6) \div (-1)$ ____ 7 **30.** $-30 \div (-5) \div (-1)$ ____ 6

31. The melting point of the metal gallium is 86°F. What is this temperature in degrees Celsius?

32. The melting point of sulfur is 120°C. What is this temperature in degrees Fahrenheit?

33. The gains and losses in the worth of a share of stock over a 5-day period are $6, $2, −$1, −$3, and $1. Find the mean change in worth of the stock over the 5-day period.

34. The low temperatures for a town during a week in January are shown in the table. Find the mean of the temperatures.

Day	Monday	Tuesday	Wednesday	Thursday	Friday	Saturday	Sunday
Temperature	−15°F	−9°F	2°F	0°F	−3°F	−5°F	2°F

Name _____ Date _____

Practice

For use with pages 301–306

Show that the number is rational by writing it in $\frac{a}{b}$ form. Then give the multiplicative inverse and the additive inverse of the number.

1. $-\frac{4}{7}$

2. $8\frac{2}{5}$

3. 0.6

4. 15

5. $-1\frac{1}{2}$

6. -0.25

Use a number line to order the rational numbers from least to greatest.

7. $-5.2, -4, -\frac{13}{3}, -4\frac{1}{2}, -5$

8. $6, -5\frac{1}{2}, 0, -\frac{8}{3}, -0.79$

9. $\frac{4}{5}, -\frac{6}{7}, 0.05, 1, -0.3$

Evaluate the expression. Justify each step you take.

10. $53 + 22 + 67$

11. $\frac{1}{4} + \frac{3}{7} + \left(-\frac{1}{4}\right)$

12. $12 \cdot \frac{2}{5} \cdot \frac{1}{12}$

13. $-4.8 + [3 + (-1.2)]$

14. $[6 \cdot (-3)] \cdot 15$

15. $4 \cdot 11 \cdot 25$

Name _____ Date _____

Practice

For use with pages 301–306

Complete the statement using <, >, or =.

16. $-\dfrac{2}{3} + \dfrac{5}{6} + \dfrac{2}{3}$ _____ 1   **17.** $\dfrac{7}{8} \cdot \dfrac{6}{1} \cdot \dfrac{8}{7}$ _____ 6   **18.** $(-18.4 + 23) + (-4.6)$ _____ 0

Evaluate the expression for the given values of the variables. Justify each step you take.

19. $a + (6.2 + b)$ when $a = 3.8$, $b = -9$

20. $\dfrac{9}{14} + a + b$ when $a = \dfrac{3}{8}$, $b = -\dfrac{9}{14}$

21. The recorded rainfall for a town for the first three months of the year are 1.36, 0.87, and 2.04. Write and simplify an expression to find the total amount of rainfall for the three months. Justify each step you take.

22. A music store sells drumsticks for $10 per pair. The store buys the drumsticks in boxes that contain 12 pairs of sticks per box. The expression $\dfrac{1}{12} \cdot 10 \cdot 12$ gives the amount of money the store will earn from selling $\dfrac{1}{12}$ of a box of drumsticks. Find the amount of money earned from selling the drumsticks. Justify each step you take.

Name _____ Date _____

Practice

For use with pages 307–311

1. Use the distributive property to write an equation for the model.

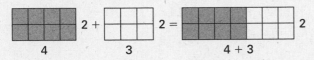

2. Describe and correct the error in using the distributive property to evaluate the expression.

$$4(25 - 3) = 4(25) - 4(-3)$$
$$= 100 + 12$$
$$= 112$$

Use the distributive property to write an equivalent expression.
Check your answer.

3. $7(6 + 4)$ **4.** $8(8 + 5)$ **5.** $9(3) + 9(5)$

6. $6(100 - 8)$ **7.** $5\left(\dfrac{13}{16}\right) - 5\left(\dfrac{5}{16}\right)$ **8.** $12\left(\dfrac{2}{3}\right) + 12\left(\dfrac{1}{3}\right)$

Name _____ Date _____

Practice

For use with pages 307–311

Use the distributive property to evaluate the expression.

9. $2(6.5) + 2(3.5)$

10. $12(3.8) + 12(1.2)$

11. $7(15.8) + 7(4.2)$

12. $15\left(\frac{3}{4}\right) + 15\left(\frac{1}{4}\right)$

13. $19\left(\frac{2}{5}\right) - 19\left(-\frac{3}{5}\right)$

14. $6(10.7)$

Use the distributive property to find the missing number or variable.

15. $b \cdot 15 + b \cdot 9 = b(15 + \underline{\quad})$

16. $14 \cdot 6 + 14 \cdot \underline{\quad} = 14(6 + y)$

17. You and three friends are taking a trip to the zoo. The zoo charges $12 for admission and you all decide to buy the $5 box lunch offered by the zoo. Use the distributive property to write two equivalent expressions to represent the total cost of the visit for your entire group. Then find the total cost for the group.

18. You buy five CDs at a sale for $5.95 each. Write an expression for the total cost of the CDs. Then use the distributive property and mental math to evaluate the expression.

19. You are carpeting two rooms in your home. One room is 7 feet long and 6 feet wide, and the other is 8 feet long and 6 feet wide. Use the distributive property to write two equivalent expressions to represent the total area of the two rooms. Then find the total area of the two rooms.

Name _____ Date _____

Practice

For use with pages 313–318

Name the ordered pair that describes the point.

1. A

2. B

3. C

4. D

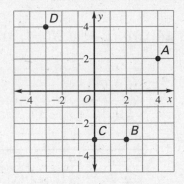

Name the ordered pair that is described by the action.

5. Point E is located 5 units to the left of the origin and 5 units above the origin.

6. Point F is located 6 units to the right of the origin and 3 units below the origin.

Plot the point and describe its location.

7. $G(4, -5)$ 8. $H(-3, -2)$ 9. $I(-4, 0)$

10. $J(-1, 2)$ 11. $K(0, 2)$ 12. $L(3, 3)$

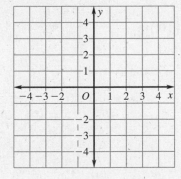

Name _____ Date _____

Practice

For use with pages 313–318

Plot and connect the points to form a rectangle. Then find the length, width, and area of the rectangle.

13. $A(0, 0)$, $B(3, 0)$, $C(3, 4)$, $D(0, 4)$

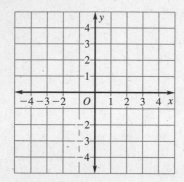

14. $W(-1, -1)$, $X(-1, 3)$, $Y(4, 3)$, $Z(4, -1)$

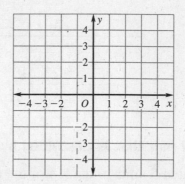

15. Make a conclusion about the scatter plot.

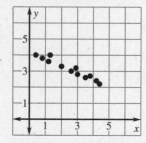

16. The ordered pairs show the heights, in inches, and the weights, in pounds, of seven American Quarter Horses. Make a scatter plot of the data. Then make a conclusion about the data.

(60.3, 950), (60.8, 1100), (60.5, 980), (61.7, 1200), (63.8, 1190), (61.4, 980), (62.6, 1140)

17. Using your results from Exercise 16, predict the weight of an American Quarter Horse that is 62 inches tall.

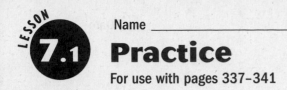

Write the verbal phrase as a variable expression. Let _x_ represent the number.

1. A number added to 10

2. 14 decreased by a number

3. 4 times a number

4. −13 increased by a number

5. 11 decreased by the quotient of 9 and a number

6. Twice a number subtracted from 1

Write the verbal sentence as an equation. Let _y_ represent the number.

7. 15 increased by a number equals 27.

8. The difference of a number and 2 is 19.

9. The sum of twice a number and 7 is 32.

10. $\frac{1}{3}$ of a number decreased by 13 equals 45.

Write a verbal phrase for the variable expression.

11. $x + 12$

12. $9 - a$

13. $m \div 5$

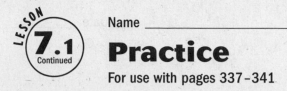

Name _____ Date _____

Practice

For use with pages 337–341

Write a verbal sentence for the equation.

14. $b - 3 = 7$ **15.** $8y = 27$ **16.** $11 + 2x = 30$

Write the real-world phrase as a variable expression. Be sure to identify what the variable represents.

17. 1 mile more than yesterday's run

18. Two times your previous high score

19. One-third of the recipe

20. 3 inches shorter than your other dog

21. Yosemite National Park has many natural waterfalls within its boundaries, including Horsetail Fall and Yosemite Falls. Horsetail Fall, which is 1000 feet tall, is 1425 feet shorter than Yosemite Falls. Write an equation to find the height of Yosemite Falls. Then use mental math to solve the equation.

22. The population of Cape Coral, Florida increased by 27 thousand people from 1990 to 2000. In 2000, the population of Cape Coral was 102 thousand people. Write an equation to find the population of Cape Coral in 1990. Then use mental math to solve the equation.

23. In 2001, the cost of mailing a letter was 17 times the cost of mailing a letter in 1885. If it cost $.34 to mail a letter in 2001, find the cost of mailing a letter in 1885.

LESSON 7.2

Practice

For use with pages 342–345

Tell whether the statement is *true* or *false*.

1. The coefficients of the expression $8 - 5x - 4 + 3x$ are 5 and 3.

2. The constants of the expression $-4 + 11x + 9 - 8x$ are -4 and 9.

3. In the expression $3x - 9 + 3 - 10x$, $3x$ and 3 are like terms.

4. The expressions $15x - 9 - 4x + 2$ and $11x - 7$ are equivalent.

Identify the coefficients, constant term(s), and like terms of the expression.

5. $8x + 9 - 3x$

6. $17 - 2a + 5a - 1$

7. $7m - 7 + 6m - 6$

8. $-10 - 15r - 22r + 8$

Match the expression with an equivalent expression.

9. $5x - 4 - 3x + 9$

10. $5(x - 3) - 3x + 7$

11. $-5x + 6 + 7x - 9$

A. $2x - 3$

B. $2x + 5$

C. $2x - 8$

Name _____ Date _____

Practice

For use with pages 342–345

Simplify the expression.

12. $18n + 13 - 5n$

13. $4x - 6 - 9x + 1$

14. $-12a - 7 + 4a + 7$

15. $-6 + 14r - 12r - 3$

16. $3(5 + 4b) - 2$

17. $6(3 - 2z) + 11z - 4$

18. A nut mixture contains peanuts, walnuts, and cashews. In the mixture, the amount of peanuts is three times the amount of cashews, and the amount of walnuts is four times the amount of cashews. Let x represent the amount of cashews. Write and simplify an expression for the total amount of nuts in the mixture.

19. A rectangular sheet of plywood is seven times longer than it is wide. Write and simplify an expression for the perimeter of the rectangle in terms of the width w.

20. A basketball player scored 8 points total during the first and second quarters of a game. During the third quarter, she scored three times as many points as she did in the fourth quarter. Let x represent the number of points the player scored in the fourth quarter. Write and simplify an expression to represent the total number of points the player scored during the entire game.

Name _____ Date _____

Practice
For use with pages 347–352

Tell whether the given value of the variable is a solution of the equation.

1. $x + 15 = 20; x = 5$ **2.** $a - 12 = 13; a = 1$ **3.** $7 + m = -31; m = 24$

Solve the equation. Check your answer.

4. $y + 6 = 15$ **5.** $n + 23 = -14$ **6.** $18 = r + 7$

7. $a - 12 = 28$ **8.** $z - 24 = -9$ **9.** $20 = s - 35$

10. $3.6 + m = 2.5$ **11.** $c - 2.1 = 6.7$ **12.** $4.2 + x - 1.4 = 7.5$

13. $t - \dfrac{1}{5} = \dfrac{3}{10}$ **14.** $\dfrac{6}{7} = a + 1$ **15.** $-\dfrac{1}{2} + x + \dfrac{2}{3} = -\dfrac{5}{6}$

16. Describe and correct the error in solving
the equation $1.8 + a = -4.5$.

$$1.8 + a = -4.5$$
$$1.8 + a - 1.8 = 4.5 - 1.8$$
$$a = 2.7$$

Write the verbal sentence as an equation. Then solve the equation.

17. The difference of a number b and 8 is -15.

18. 9 more than a number x is 24.

Name _____ Date _____

Practice

For use with pages 347–352

Write and solve an equation to find the unknown side length.

19. Perimeter: 12 ft

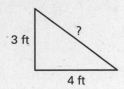

20. Perimeter: 11.3 mm

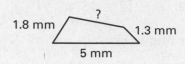

21. Perimeter: 12.3 in.

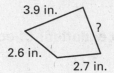

22. A paperback version of a book costs $17.10. This cost is $2.89 less than the cost of the hardcover version of the book. Write and solve an equation to find the hardcover cost of the book.

23. During a recent trip to the gym, you worked out with free weights and rode a stationary bike. You used a stationary bike for 28 minutes of the 75 minutes you spent at the gym. Write and solve an equation to find the number of minutes you spent working out with free weights.

24. The left- and right-hand margins on a sheet of paper are both 1.25 inches wide. The total width of the sheet of paper is 8.5 inches. Write and solve an equation to find the width of the text area that lies between the margins.

Name _____ Date _____

Practice

For use with pages 354–359

Tell whether the given value of the variable is a solution of the equation.

1. $-5r = 125; r = -15$ **2.** $4.2a = -21; a = -5$ **3.** $\dfrac{n}{-6} = -84; n = -14$

Describe how to solve the equation without actually solving.

4. $8x = 72$ **5.** $-14b = 8$ **6.** $\dfrac{m}{11} = -6$

Solve the equation. Check your solution. Round the solution to the nearest hundredth if necessary.

7. $4p = 48$ **8.** $2.3y = -20.7$ **9.** $-\dfrac{1}{5}c = 35$

10. $-9d = -76.5$ **11.** $\dfrac{m}{7} = -43$ **12.** $\dfrac{z}{6.2} = 4.5$

13. $\dfrac{a}{-8} = 3.6$ **14.** $-9.8 = \dfrac{w}{-2.3}$ **15.** $-6 = \dfrac{3}{8}r$

16. $\dfrac{5}{3}t = 30$ **17.** $5.3q = 1.431$ **18.** $b + 4b = 8$

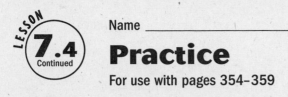
Name _____ Date _____

Practice

For use with pages 354–359

Write the verbal sentence as an equation. Then solve the equation.

19. The quotient of a number x and 6 is 8.7.

20. Three times a number a equals 14.4.

21. The product of -2.2 and a number m is 13.2.

22. At a part-time job, Marcus earns $8.50 per hour. Write and solve
an equation to find the number of hours he has to work to earn $102.

23. It costs you $1.96 for four pounds of bananas. Write and solve an
equation to find the cost of one pound of bananas.

24. In a survey about favorite book categories, $\frac{1}{4}$ of the total number
of people surveyed, or 39 people, responded that mystery was their
favorite category. Write and solve an equation to find the total
number of people surveyed.

Name _____ Date _____

Practice

For use with pages 361–365

Tell whether the given value of the variable is a solution of the equation.

1. $6x - 5 = 13; x = 3$ **2.** $8m + 7 = -17; m = 3$ **3.** $3c - 1 = -4; c = -1$

Match the equation with its solution.

4. $4y - 3 = -1$ **A.** $y = -1$

5. $-3y + 4 = -1$ **B.** $y = \dfrac{1}{2}$

6. $-4y - 3 = 1$ **C.** $y = 1$

7. $3y - 4 = -1$ **D.** $y = 1\dfrac{2}{3}$

8. Put the steps for solving the equation $9x - 8 = -5$ in order.

    A. Divide each side by 9.   **B.** Write original equation.

    C. Check your answer.   **D.** Add 8 to each side.

Solve the equation. Check your solution.

9. $7a + 4 = -17$ **10.** $-5s - 13 = -68$ **11.** $12 - x = 19$

12. $\dfrac{n}{6} - 4 = 4$ **13.** $\dfrac{d}{3.2} + 6 = 21$ **14.** $\dfrac{1}{2}p - 7 = -27$

15. $0 = 14t + 26$ **16.** $\dfrac{3}{4}m - 5 = 16$ **17.** $3.4c - 1.7 = 6.8$

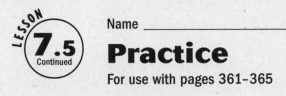

LESSON
7.5
Continued

Name _____ Date _____

Practice

For use with pages 361–365

Write the verbal sentence as an equation. Then solve the equation.

18. Twice the number r increased by 15 equals -17.

19. 8 subtracted from 3 times a number c is 31.

20. A mail-order CD company is advertising a sale. During the sale, CDs are $6.95 each and the shipping and handling charge is only $5.25. How many CDs can you buy for $40?

21. A window is 21 inches wide, and its perimeter is 112 inches. What is the length of the window?

22. Kathy earns $445 a week for 40 hours of work and $25 an hour for each hour over 40. How many hours did Kathy work if she earned $570 in one week?

Name _____ Date _____

Practice

For use with pages 366–370

Tell whether the given value of the variable is a solution of the inequality.

1. $x - 7 \le -5$; $x = -8$　　　　**2.** $4a \ge 36$; $a = 9$　　　　**3.** $-3m < 4$; $m = -\dfrac{3}{2}$

Write an inequality represented by the graph.

4.
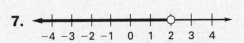

5.

6.

7.

8. Describe and correct the error in finding the solution to $8p \ge -7$.

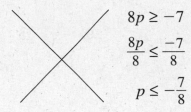

$$8p \ge -7$$
$$\frac{8p}{8} \le \frac{-7}{8}$$
$$p \le -\frac{7}{8}$$

Write an inequality to represent the situation. Then graph the inequality.

9. To ride an amusement park ride, you must be 48 inches tall or taller.

10. A restaurant can hold at most 40 people.

11. To run for the President of the United States, you must be at least 35 years old.

Name _____ Date _____

Practice

For use with pages 366–370

Solve the inequality. Then graph the solution.

12. $x + 8 < 15$

13. $c - 12 \geq -38$

14. $m - 24 \leq -30$

15. $14 + r > 43$

16. $-63 + w \geq 120$

17. $-5a < 20$

18. $\dfrac{x}{8} \geq \dfrac{1}{4}$

19. $\dfrac{n}{-3} > 15$

20. $\dfrac{2}{3}q < -18$

21. A wheelbarrow can carry at most 400 pounds. Write and solve an inequality to find the greatest number of 50-pound bags of concrete that the wheelbarrow can carry.

22. A book store sells used paperbacks for $3.75 each. You receive a $2 discount if you spend at least $30 in the store. Write and solve an inequality that represents the least number of paperbacks you must buy in order to receive the discount.

23. You are mailing a 42-pound item by parcel post. The total weight of an item and its packaging cannot be greater than 70 pounds. Write and solve an inequality that represents the heaviest the packaging can be without exceeding the 70-pound weight limit.

Name _____ Date _____

Practice

For use with pages 371–375

Evaluate the function $y = 5x - 3$ for the given value of x.

1. 7

2. 0

3. -4

Match the function with its possible range when the domain is $-2, -1, 0, 1, 2$.

4. $y = 2x - 1$

5. $y = -x + 2$

6. $y = 3x - 1$

7. $y = -5x + 1$

A. $-7, -4, -1, 2, 5$

B. $-5, -3, -1, 1, 3$

C. $11, 6, 1, -4, -9$

D. $4, 3, 2, 1, 0$

Make an input-output table for the function using the domain $-2, -1, 0, 1,$ and 2. Then state the range of the function.

8. $y = x + 8$

9. $y = -15x$

10. $y = 4.3x$

11. $y = x - 2.75$

12. $y = 0.4x - 3$

13. $y = 18 - 3x$

LESSON
7.7
Continued

Name _____ Date _____

Practice

For use with pages 371–375

Write a function rule for the input-output table.

14.

Input x	0	1	2	3
Output y	3	4	5	6

15.

Input x	0	1	2	3
Output y	5	4	3	2

16.

Input x	−3	−2	−1	0
Output y	−12	−8	−4	0

17.

Input x	0	1	2	3
Output y	1.2	2.2	3.2	4.2

18. A custom case company makes travel cases for computer equipment. There is a 2-inch foam lining around the inside of each case. The function $y = x + 4$, where x is the width of a laptop computer, can be used to find the total width of a laptop case, including the foam lining. Create an input-output table using the domain 12, 15, 18, and 21.

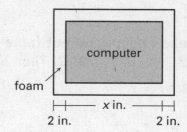

19. A magazine costs $3.95 per issue. Write a function rule that models the cost y of x issues. Then use the function to calculate the cost of 6 issues.

20. It costs $.15 to make one copy on the copier at the local library. Write a function rule that models the cost y of making x copies. Then use the function to calculate the cost of 24 copies.

Name _____ Date _____

7.8 Practice

For use with pages 376–381

Identify the graph of the function on the coordinate plane.

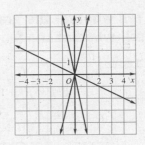

1. $y = -5x$

2. $y = 4x$

3. $y = -\frac{1}{2}x$

Graph the function.

4. $y = 3x$

5. $y = 8 - x$

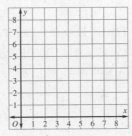

6. $y = \frac{1}{4}x$

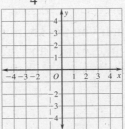

7. $y = x + 5$

8. $y = 3x - 6$

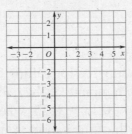

9. $y = -2x + 3$

10. $y = \frac{1}{3}x + 2$

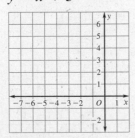

11. $y = 0.75x - 3$

12. $y = -x - 8$

Write and graph a function that converts the units.

13. x feet to y inches

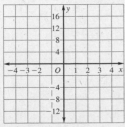

14. x pounds to y ounces

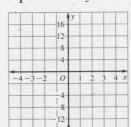

15. x months to y years

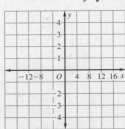

Name _____ Date _____

Practice

For use with pages 376–381

Tell whether the graph represents a function of _x_. If it does, tell whether the function is _linear_ or _nonlinear_.

16.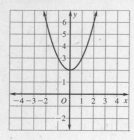

17.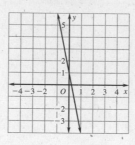

18.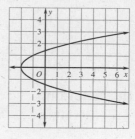

19. When you are swimming, your body burns about 8 calories every minute. Write and graph a function that models the number of calories burned _y_ after swimming for _x_ minutes.

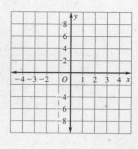

20. Outdoor carpeting costs $1.25 for each square foot. Write and graph a function that models the cost _y_ of _x_ square feet of carpeting.

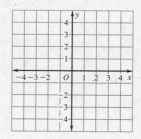

21. A phone company charges a $.25 dialing fee for calling a long-distance number and then charges $.10 for each minute of the call. This situation can be represented by the function $y = 0.1x + 0.25$, where _y_ is the total cost of the call and _x_ is the length of the call in minutes. Graph the function.

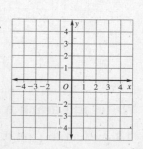

LESSON 8.1 Practice

For use with pages 399–403

Match the statement with its ratio.

1. shaded squares to unshaded squares

2. unshaded squares to total squares

3. total squares to shaded squares

A. 20 : 8

B. 8 : 12

C. 12 : 20

The table shows the numbers of wins and losses for two little league baseball teams during a season. Use the table to write the specified ratio.

	Wins	Losses
Dynamos	13	17
Titans	19	11

4. Dynamos wins to Titans wins

5. Titans wins to Titans losses

6. Dynamos losses to all Dynamos games

Write the ratio as a fraction in simplest form.

7. $\dfrac{9}{27}$

8. $\dfrac{18}{24}$

9. 4 : 70

10. 35 to 105

11. 22 : 7

12. 12 to 165

Write the ratio of the first measurement to the second measurement. Write both measurements in the same unit.

13. 84 ft, 54 in.

14. 2 h, 150 min

15. 14 mm, 3 cm

Name _____ Date _____

Practice

For use with pages 399–403

Complete the statement using <, >, or =.

16. $8:10$ ____ $4:12$ **17.** $45:36$ ____ $15:12$ **18.** $54:78$ ____ $64:84$

Find a value for x that makes the first ratio equivalent to the second ratio.

19. x to 5, 80 to 25 **20.** x to 14, 56 to 98 **21.** x to 117, 4 to 9

22. The Roanoke River is 410 miles long, but boats can only travel on, or navigate, 112 miles of the total length. Write the ratio of the Roanoke's navigable length to its total length as a fraction in simplest form.

23. There were 128 threatened species of animals and 144 threatened species of plants in the United States in 2001. Write the ratio of threatened species of animals to threatened species of plants as a fraction in simplest form.

24. In the 2000 Summer Olympics, Australia earned 16 gold medals, 25 silver medals, and 17 bronze medals. Write the ratio of gold medals to all medals as a fraction in simplest form.

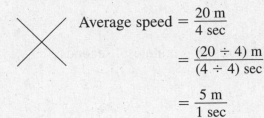

1. Describe and correct the error in finding the average speed for an object traveling 4 meters in 20 seconds.

$$\text{Average speed} = \frac{20 \text{ m}}{4 \text{ sec}}$$

$$= \frac{(20 \div 4) \text{ m}}{(4 \div 4) \text{ sec}}$$

$$= \frac{5 \text{ m}}{1 \text{ sec}}$$

Match the rate with the equivalent unit rate.

2. $\frac{42 \text{ m}}{15 \text{ sec}}$ **3.** $\frac{72 \text{ m}}{8 \text{ sec}}$ **4.** $\frac{13 \text{ m}}{4 \text{ sec}}$

A. $\frac{2.8 \text{ m}}{1 \text{ sec}}$ **B.** $\frac{3.25 \text{ m}}{1 \text{ sec}}$ **C.** $\frac{9 \text{ m}}{1 \text{ sec}}$

Find the unit rate.

5. $\frac{16 \text{ L}}{2 \text{ h}}$ **6.** $\frac{\$54}{6 \text{ lb}}$

7. $\frac{18 \text{ ft}}{5 \text{ sec}}$ **8.** \$28 for 8 people

9. 17 ounces for \$5   **10.** 30 cups for 16 servings

Name _____ Date _____

Practice

For use with pages 404–408

Find the average speed.

11. 128 inches in 16 hours

12. 34 meters in 10 seconds

13. 384 feet in 4 minutes 16 seconds

14. 184 yards in 3 minutes 4 seconds

Determine which is the better buy.

15. Salsa: 16 ounces for $3.36 or 24 ounces for $4.80

16. Mustard: 12 ounces for $1.56 or 18 ounces for $2.70

17. Milk: 2 quarts for $3 or 4 quarts for $5.96

18. The gas mileage of a car is the ratio of the number of miles driven to the number of gallons of gasoline used. You use 3 gallons of gasoline to drive a car 84 miles. Write the gas mileage of the car as a unit rate.

19. A person's hourly earnings can be described as the ratio of the amount of money earned to the number of hours worked. Wendy earns $450 for working 36 hours in one week. Write her hourly earnings as a unit rate.

20. A swimmer completed a 150-meter race in 1 minute and 40 seconds. What was the swimmer's average speed?

Name _____ Date _____

Practice

For use with pages 409–414

Without finding the slope of the line, tell whether the slope is
positive, *negative*, or *zero*.

1.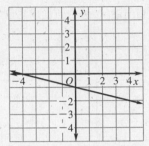

2.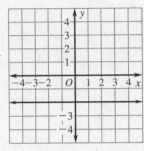

3.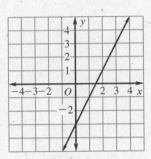

Find the slope of the line.

4.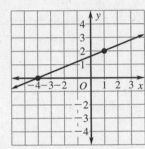

5.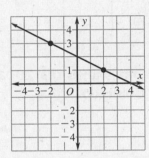

6.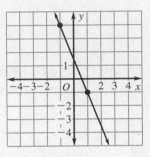

Draw the graph of the line that passes through the points.
Then find the slope of the line.

7. $(4, 1), (5, 2)$

8. $(0, 0), (3, -4)$

9. $(-2, 5), (1, -2)$

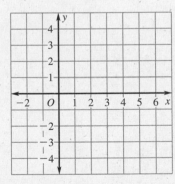

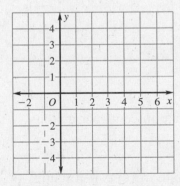

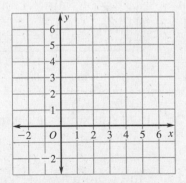

10. $(-3, -1), (2, -4)$

11. $(5, 1), (-2, 2)$

12. $(-2, 3), (-5, -2)$

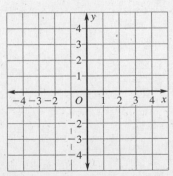

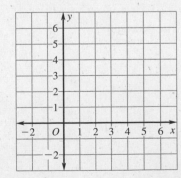

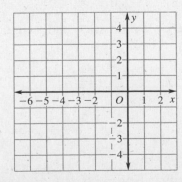

Name _____ Date _____

Practice

For use with pages 409-414

Draw the line that has the given slope and passes through the given point.

13. slope = 2; (−4, 1)   **14.** slope = $\frac{2}{3}$; (4, 1)   **15.** slope = $−\frac{1}{2}$; (0, 3)

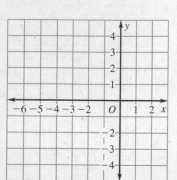   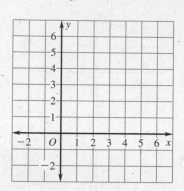   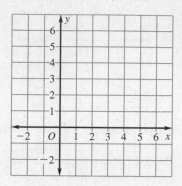

In Exercises 16–18, use the graph that shows the 2001 state gasoline tax rates for Alabama and Colorado.

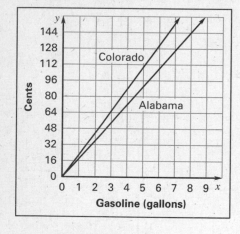

16. Find Alabama's gasoline tax rate in cents per gallon.

17. Find Colorado's gasoline tax rate in cents per gallon.

18. Which state had a higher gasoline tax rate?

Name _____ Date _____

Practice

For use with pages 418–422

Use equivalent ratios to solve the proportion.

1. $\dfrac{x}{21} = \dfrac{6}{7}$

2. $\dfrac{3}{b} = \dfrac{24}{88}$

3. $\dfrac{18}{81} = \dfrac{p}{9}$

4. $\dfrac{33}{45} = \dfrac{11}{r}$

5. $\dfrac{y}{13} = \dfrac{60}{156}$

6. $\dfrac{18}{14} = \dfrac{c}{21}$

Use algebra to solve the proportion.

7. $\dfrac{z}{7} = \dfrac{16}{56}$

8. $\dfrac{24}{a} = \dfrac{6}{9}$

9. $\dfrac{16}{40} = \dfrac{q}{5}$

10. $\dfrac{18}{72} = \dfrac{s}{4}$

11. $\dfrac{w}{16} = \dfrac{35}{40}$

12. $\dfrac{48}{20} = \dfrac{12}{d}$

13. Two pounds of apples cost \$3. Describe and correct the error in the proportion used to find the cost c of 18 pounds of apples.

$\times \quad \dfrac{2}{3} = \dfrac{c}{18}$

Name _____ Date _____

Practice

For use with pages 418–422

Write and then solve the proportion.

14. 9 is to 2 as x is to 16.

15. 6 is to 20 as 54 is to b.

16. m is to 18 as 5 is to 90.

17. 100 is to 75 as 4 is to r.

18. In 2000, the average television viewer watched about 29 hours of television in 7 days. About how many hours of television did the average viewer watch in 28 days?

19. Carbon is one of the building blocks of human cells. A 150-pound person's body contains 27 pounds of carbon. Assuming that the ratio of the number of pounds of carbon in a person to his or her weight is the same for every person, how many pounds of carbon are in a 120-pound person?

20. A recipe that makes 8 pints of coleslaw uses 2 heads of cabbage. How many pints of coleslaw can be made from 5 heads of cabbage?

21. A modem transfers 512 kilobytes of data in 4 seconds. At this rate, how long does it take to transfer 7680 kilobytes of data?

Name _____ Date _____

Practice

For use with pages 423–428

Use the cross products property to solve the proportion.

1. $\dfrac{x}{6} = \dfrac{6}{4}$

2. $\dfrac{8}{2} = \dfrac{24}{b}$

3. $\dfrac{18}{t} = \dfrac{3}{5}$

4. $\dfrac{3}{7} = \dfrac{q}{28}$

5. $\dfrac{y}{6.6} = \dfrac{5}{11}$

6. $\dfrac{3}{5.5} = \dfrac{6}{d}$

7. $\dfrac{2}{n} = \dfrac{40}{65}$

8. $\dfrac{1}{4} = \dfrac{c}{17}$

9. $\dfrac{15.2}{19} = \dfrac{z}{2.5}$

10. Describe and correct the error in solving the proportion $\dfrac{3}{5} = \dfrac{x}{24}$.

$$\frac{3}{5} = \frac{x}{24}$$

$$3 \cdot x = 5 \cdot 24$$

$$x = 40$$

Write and then solve the proportion.

11. 21 is to y as 7 is to 15.

12. 2.4 is to 3.6 as x is to 12.

13. 14 is to 6 as m is to 10.2.

14. 3.2 is to 4.1 as 9.6 is to p.

Practice

For use with pages 423–428

Tell whether the ratios form a proportion.

15. $\dfrac{20}{75}, \dfrac{4}{15}$

16. $\dfrac{8}{9}, \dfrac{36}{32}$

17. $\dfrac{1.2}{3.4}, \dfrac{6}{17}$

18. Leslie can read about 2192 words in 8 minutes. About how many words can she read in 60 minutes?

19. The national flag of France has a width-to-length ratio of 2 : 3. What is the width of an 18-inch long French flag?

20. A filter for an aquarium cleans 800 gallons of water in 60 minutes. How many gallons of water does the filter clean in 4.5 minutes?

21. There are 2 grams of fiber in 0.25 cup of raisins. How many cups of raisins are needed to get 5 grams of fiber?

Name _____ Date _____

Practice

For use with pages 430–435

**The scale on a map is 1 cm : 12 km. Find the actual distance
in kilometers for the given length on the map.**

1. 4 cm

2. 7.25 cm

3. 11.25 cm

**Models of buildings in Detroit, Michigan were created by using a
scale of 1 in. : 50 ft. Find the height of the model in inches for
the given height of the building.**

4. Marriott Hotel: 725 ft

5. Book Tower: 472 ft

6. Madden Building: 470 ft

7. ANR Building: 430 ft

8. Which scale is equivalent to 1 cm : 25 m?

A. 1 : 25

B. 1 : 2500

C. 1 : 25,000

Name _____ Date _____

Practice
For use with pages 430–435

Find the scale used to create the model.

9. The scale model of a 72-inch long table is 8 inches long.

10. The scale model of an 84-inch long couch is 7 inches long.

11. The scale model of a 45-inch tall bookcase is 2.5 inches tall.

12. The scale model of a 40-inch tall chair is 1.25 inches tall.

Write the scale so that the units are the same.

13. 1 in. : 12 ft

14. 1 cm : 15 m

15. 1 in. : 25 yd

16. The table shows some common scales used in model railroading.
For each scale, find the length of a model of an 82-foot long boxcar.
Give the length of each model in inches.

Scale Name	Scale
N	1 : 160
S	1 : 64
O	1 : 48

17. The scale 1 in. : 120 ft was used to create a 169.3-inch tall model of
Alaska's Mount McKinley. Estimate the height of Mount McKinley
from the height of the model.

LESSON 9.1

Practice

For use with pages 449–452

Write the percent as a fraction.

1. 88%

2. 48%

3. 10%

4. 75%

5. 2%

6. 39%

Write the fraction as a percent.

7. $\frac{4}{5}$

8. $\frac{3}{10}$

9. $\frac{29}{50}$

10. $\frac{9}{20}$

11. $\frac{14}{25}$

12. $\frac{1}{5}$

Find the percent of the number.

13. 40% of 85

14. 25% of 64

15. 10% of 150

16. 70% of 30

17. 50% of 400

18. 15% of 200

Name _____ Date _____

Practice
For use with pages 449–452

Tell whether the statement is *true* or *false*. If it is false, correct the statement.

19. $\dfrac{1}{10} = 1\%$

20. $\dfrac{43}{50} = 86\%$

21. $\dfrac{17}{20} = 34\%$

Solve the proportion by writing the fraction as a percent.

22. $\dfrac{7}{20} = \dfrac{x}{100}$

23. $\dfrac{21}{25} = \dfrac{y}{100}$

24. $\dfrac{33}{50} = \dfrac{v}{100}$

Complete the statement using <, >, or =.

25. 20% of 90 _____ 25% of 100

26. 12% of 350 _____ 12% of 250

27. Only 40% of people between the ages of 18 and 24 read a daily newspaper. Write the percent as a fraction in simplest form.

28. Seven out of every 20 homes that own at least one television have two televisions. What percent of the homes that own at least one television have two televisions?

29. Five of the 100 seniors at your school are on the yearbook staff. What percent of your school's seniors are not on the yearbook staff?

Name _____ Date _____

Practice

For use with pages 454–459

Complete the proportion. Then answer the question.

1. What number is 75% of 320?

$$\frac{a}{\underline{\quad}} = \frac{}{100}$$

2. What percent of 40 is 4?

$$\frac{}{\underline{\quad}} = \frac{p}{100}$$

3. Describe and correct the error when using a proportion to answer the question.

   50 is 20% of what number?

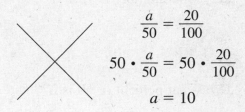

$$\frac{a}{50} = \frac{20}{100}$$

$$50 \cdot \frac{a}{50} = 50 \cdot \frac{20}{100}$$

$$a = 10$$

Match the question with the correct proportion.

4. 75 is 12% of what number?

A. $\frac{12}{75} = \frac{p}{100}$

5. What number is 12% of 75?

B. $\frac{75}{b} = \frac{12}{100}$

6. What percent of 75 is 12?

C. $\frac{a}{75} = \frac{12}{100}$

Name _____ Date _____

Practice

For use with pages 454–459

Use a proportion to answer the question.

7. What percent of 50 is 5?   **8.** What percent of 75 is 21?

9. 68 is 85% of what number?   **10.** 40 is 32% of what number?

11. What number is 15% of 80?   **12.** What number is 40% of 95?

13. What percent of 60 is 27?   **14.** 18 is 6% of what number?

Write the fraction as a percent. Round your answer to the nearest whole percent.

15. $\frac{1}{9}$ **16.** $\frac{2}{11}$ **17.** $\frac{3}{13}$

18. You have 45 books on your bookshelf. If 9 are mystery books, what percent of the books on your bookshelf are mystery books?

19. Five percent of Ireland's total area is forest and woodland. The total area of Ireland is 70,280 square kilometers. How many square kilometers of Ireland's area are forest and woodland?

20. Forty-five percent of the trees in a park are maple trees. There are 27 maple trees in the park. How many trees are in the park in all?

Name _____ Date _____

Practice

For use with pages 460–464

Draw a model for the percent.

1. 44%   **2.** 4.5%   **3.** 112%

Write the percent as a decimal.

4. 34%   **5.** 2%

6. 175%   **7.** 0.8%

8. 27.9%   **9.** 6.25%

Write the decimal as a percent.

10. 0.29   **11.** 0.05

12. 0.308   **13.** 4.132

14. 17.04   **15.** 0.00688

Name _____ Date _____

Practice

For use with pages 460–464

Write the fraction as a percent. Round to the nearest tenth of a percent.

16. $\dfrac{7}{18}$

17. $\dfrac{15}{21}$

18. $\dfrac{5}{34}$

19. $\dfrac{24}{45}$

20. $\dfrac{13}{54}$

21. $\dfrac{22}{95}$

Complete the statement using <, >, or =.

22. 0.25% ____ 0.025

23. 8.1 ____ 81%

24. 0.034 ____ 3.4%

25. In 1960, a farmer was paid $1 for one bushel of corn. In 2000, the price of one bushel of corn was 185% of the 1960 price. How much was a farmer paid for one bushel of corn in 2000?

26. About 0.6% of Nebraska's total area is water. The total area of Nebraska is 77,354 square miles. How many square miles of Nebraska's total area is water?

27. The cost of airmailing a 60-ounce package to Mexico is 3050% of the cost of airmailing a 1-ounce package to Mexico. It costs $.60 to airmail a 1-ounce package. How much does it cost to airmail a 60-ounce package?

LESSON 9.4 Practice

For use with pages 465–470

Match the question with the correct equation.

1. 94 is 17% of what number?   **A.** $a = 0.17 \cdot 94$

2. What percent of 94 is 17?   **B.** $94 = 0.17 \cdot b$

3. What number is 17% of 94?   **C.** $17 = p\% \cdot 94$

4. Which expression would you use to estimate 36% of 84?

   A. 30% of 84

   B. 25% of 84

   C. 40% of 84

   D. 35% of 84

Use the percent equation to answer the question.

5. What number is 25% of 600?   6. What number is 70% of 180?

7. 174 is what percent of 600?   8. 12 is what percent of 80?

9. 52 is what percent of 80?   10. 28 is 28% of what number?

11. 90 is 8% of what number?   12. What number is 52% of 500?

13. 178 is what percent of 200?   14. 45 is 60% of what number?

Practice

For use with pages 465–470

15. Which is greater, 35% of 60 or 30% of 80?

16. In 2000, the population of Ohio was about 4% of the population of the entire United States. The population of the United States in 2000 was about 281,422,000 people. What was Ohio's population in 2000?

17. In 2000, there were 7689 weekly newspapers in the United States. This is about 94% of the number of weekly newspapers in the United States in 1960. How many weekly newspapers were there in 1960? Round your answer to the nearest whole number.

18. In 2000, there were about 2,172,000 farms in the United States. Twenty-four thousand of the farms were in South Carolina. What percent of the farms were in South Carolina? Round your answer to the nearest whole percent.

Practice

For use with pages 474–478

In Exercises 1–3, use the circle graph that shows the results of a survey that asked students to name their favorite pet.

1. What percent of students named dogs or cats as their favorite pet?

2. What percent of students did not name fish as their favorite pet?

3. Find the angle measure of the section that represents the students who named dogs as their favorite pet.

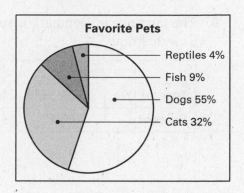

Favorite Pets

Reptiles 4%
Fish 9%
Dogs 55%
Cats 32%

Display the data in a circle graph.

4.

Getting to School	Students
Walk	30%
Ride bicycle	25%
Ride bus	40%
Ride with parents	5%

5.

Favorite Shirt	Students
T-shirt	25%
Sweater	35%
Button-down	30%
Sweatshirt	10%

6.

Favorite Juice	People
Apple	6
Grape	14
Orange	18
Pineapple	2

7.

Collecting Items	People
Baseball cards	44
Stamps	8
Coins	16
Dolls	12

Name _____ Date _____

Practice

For use with pages 474–478

8. The land use in Denmark is shown below. Display the data in a circle graph.

Denmark Land Use				
Type of Use	Arable land	Meadows and pastures	Forest and woodland	Other
Percent	60%	5%	10%	25%

Match the percent of a circle with its corresponding angle measure.

9. 17.5%   **A.** 81°

10. 22.5%   **B.** 117°

11. 32.5%   **C.** 63°

Name _____ Date _____

Practice

For use with pages 480–484

Match the situation with the correct percent of increase or percent of decrease.

1. Original: 40
New: 52

2. Original: 40
New: 28

3. Original: 40
New: 50

4. Original: 40
New: 30

A. 25% increase   **B.** 30% increase   **C.** 25% decrease   **D.** 30% decrease

Identify the percent of change as an *increase* or a *decrease*. Then find the percent of change. Use estimation to check your answer.

5. Original: 60
New: 105

6. Original: 80
New: 56

7. Original: 175
New: 420

8. Original: 1260
New: 1386

9. Original: 56
New: 70

10. Original: 195
New: 117

11. Original: 2400
New: 120

12. Original: 20
New: 21

13. Original: 225
New: 360

14. Describe and correct the error in finding a 95% increase of 140.

New amount = 95% of 140

= 0.95 × 140

= 133

Name _____ Date _____

Practice

For use with pages 480–484

Find the new amount using the given information.

15. a 28% increase of 150   **16.** a 70% decrease of 270   **17.** a 40% decrease of 85

18. a 120% increase of 95   **19.** a 13% increase of 600   **20.** an 85% decrease of 20

21. The number of visits to the Black Canyon of the Gunnison National Park in Colorado dropped from 200,000 in 1999 to 192,000 in 2000. What was the percent of decrease?

22. Arizona's population increased from 3,665,000 people in 1990 to 5,131,000 people in 2000. What was the percent of increase?

23. The number of pieces of Parcel Post mail handled by the U.S. Postal Service increased by about 70% from 1990 to 2000. The U.S. Postal Service handled 663 million pieces of Parcel Post mail in 1990. How many pieces of Parcel Post mail did they handle in 2000?

LESSON 9.7

Name _____ Date _____

Practice

For use with pages 485–489

1. Which expression will give the new price of a $15 item marked up by 28%?

   A. $28 + 0.15 \times 28$

   B. $28 - 0.15 \times 28$

   C. $15 + 0.28 \times 15$

   D. $15 - 0.28 \times 15$

Use the given information to find the new price.

2. Original price: $42
   Discount: 15%

3. Original price: $62
   Discount: 30%

4. Wholesale price: $120
   Markup: 10%

5. Wholesale price: $225
   Markup: 18%

6. Food bill before tax: $24
   Sales tax: 6%

7. Food bill before tip: $35
   Tip: 18%

8. Original price: $78
   Discount: 12%

9. Wholesale price: $218
   Markup: 33%

10. Food bill before tax: $54
    Sales tax: 7%

11. Describe and correct the error in finding the total cost of a $49 meal
    with 6% sales tax and an 18% tip.

Total cost = $49 + (0.6 + 0.18)(49)$

= $49 + (0.78)(49)$

= 87.22

Practice

For use with pages 485–489

Find the percent discount or the percent markup.

12. An item that was $25 is now $23.75.

13. An item that was $38 is now $45.60.

14. An item that was $75 is now $50.25.

15. You buy two DVDs at the video store. One DVD is $21.49 and the other DVD is $19.99, but is on sale for 15% off the original price. How much do you spend on both DVDs? Round your answer to the nearest cent.

16. The markup on a digital camera is 125%. The wholesale price of the digital camera is $97. What is the retail price?

17. At a restaurant, you order a lunch that costs $6.50 and a beverage that costs $1.50. You leave a 20% tip and the sales tax is 7%. What is the total cost?

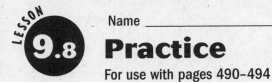
Name _____ Date _____

Practice

For use with pages 490–494

1. Which expression could be used to find the balance of an account that started with $115 and earned 4% simple annual interest for 8 months?

    A. $115 + (115)(0.04)(8)$

    B. $115 + (115)(4)(8)$

    C. $115 + (115)(0.04)\left(\frac{8}{12}\right)$

For an account that earns simple annual interest, find the interest and the balance of the account.

2. $375 at 4% for 5 years

3. $278 at 8% for 9 months

4. $2300 at 2.2% for 6 months

5. $4880 at 3.8% for 3 months

6. $1800 at 13.5% for 4 months

7. $600 at 4.5% for 24 months

8. Describe and correct the error in finding the amount of time it takes $1400 to earn $350 in interest at a 10% interest rate.

$$1400 = (350)(0.1)t$$

$$\frac{1400}{(350)(0.1)} = t$$

$$40 = t$$

Name _____ Date _____

Practice

For use with pages 490–494

Use the simple interest formula to find the unknown quantity.

9. $I =$ _____
    $P = \$4000$
    $r = 4.5\%$
    $t = 5$ years

10. $I = \$67.50$
    $P =$ _____
    $r = 3\%$
    $t = 3$ years

11. $I = \$1104$
    $P = \$4600$
    $r =$ _____
    $t = 4$ years

12. $I = \$3621.20$
    $P = \$8230$
    $r = 5.5\%$
    $t =$ _____

13. $I =$ _____
    $P = \$378$
    $r = 2\%$
    $t = 6$ years

14. $I = \$13.98$
    $P =$ _____
    $r = 3.6\%$
    $t = 4$ months

15. You deposit $425 into a money market account for three months. The account earns 2.5% simple interest. How much money is in the account after three months? Round your answer to the nearest cent.

16. You put $1000 into a six-month certificate of deposit. After the six-month period, your balance is $1012.50. What was the simple annual interest rate?

17. You deposit $4000 into a savings account. The account earns 2.75% simple interest. How long will it take to earn $220 in interest?

Name _____ Date _____

Practice

For use with pages 511–515

Estimate to classify the angle as *acute, right, obtuse,* **or** *straight.*

1.

2.

3.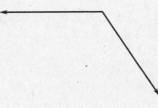

Tell whether the angles are *complementary, supplementary,* **or** *neither.* **Explain your reasoning.**

4.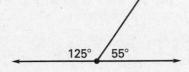

5.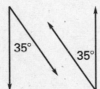

6.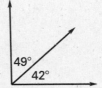

For the given angle measure, find the measure of a supplementary angle and the measure of a complementary angle, if possible.

7. 17°

8. 86°

9. 134°

10. 59°

11. 111°

12. 4°

Name _____ Date _____

Practice

For use with pages 511–515

Find the measure of the angle.

13. ∠R and ∠S are supplementary. If $m\angle R = 65°$, what is $m\angle S$?

14. ∠U and ∠V are complementary. If $m\angle U = 28°$, what is $m\angle V$?

15. The angle between the shaft of a golf club and the golf club face is called the *loft angle*. The diagram shows a club with a 44° loft angle. What is the value of x?

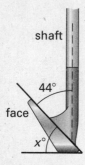

shaft

44°

face

x°

16. Sometimes ropes are tied around a tree so that it grows straight upward. The rope makes a 23° angle with the ground. What is the value of y?

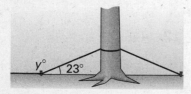

y° 23°

Name _____ Date _____

10.2 Practice

For use with pages 516–520

In Exercises 1–4, refer to the diagram.

1. Name all pairs of adjacent, supplementary angles.

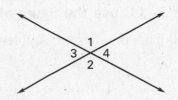

2. Name all pairs of vertical angles.

3. Given that $m\angle 1 = 123°$, find $m\angle 4$.

4. Given that $m\angle 1 = 123°$, find $m\angle 2$.

Tell whether the dark lines appear to be *parallel*, *perpendicular*, or *neither*.

5.

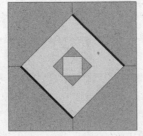

6.

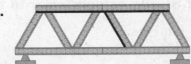

7.

Name _____ Date _____

Practice

For use with pages 516–520

**Scaffolding is used by builders to safely work on tall structures.
In Exercises 8–11, use the figure of the scaffolding.**

8. Name all pairs of adjacent, supplementary angles.

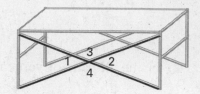

9. Name all pairs of vertical angles.

10. Given that $m\angle 1 = 42°$, find $m\angle 4$.

11. Given that $m\angle 1 = 42°$, find $m\angle 2$.

**In Exercises 12–17, refer to the street map. 4th St., 5th St., and 6th St. run parallel to
each other. Grant St. and Tyler St. run perpendicular to these streets.**

12. Find $m\angle 1$.

13. Find $m\angle 2$.

14. Find $m\angle 3$.

15. Find $m\angle 4$.

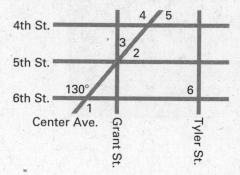

16. Find $m\angle 5$.

17. Find $m\angle 6$.

10.3 Practice

For use with pages 521–526

Find the value of *x* in the triangle shown.

1.

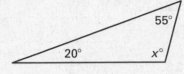

55°
20°   *x*°

2.

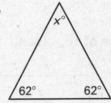

x°
62°   62°

3.

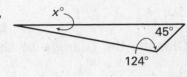

x°
45°
124°

The measures of two of the angles in a triangle are given.
Find the measure of the third angle.

4. 126.5° and 19°

5. 65.5° and 85°

6. 110.3° and 35.7°

Find the value of *y*.

7.

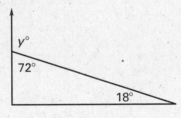

y°
72°
18°

8.

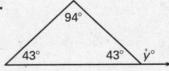

94°
43°   43°   *y*°

9.

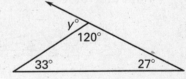

y°
120°
33°   27°

Name _____ Date _____

Practice

For use with pages 521–526

Classify the triangle by its angle measures.

10. 43°, 47°, 90°   **11.** 46°, 78°, 56°   **12.** 62°, 23°, 95°

Classify the triangle by the lengths of its sides.

13.
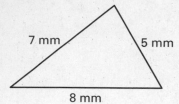
7 mm   5 mm
8 mm

14.
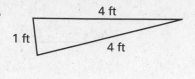
4 ft
1 ft
4 ft

15.
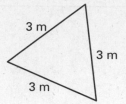
3 m
3 m
3 m
3 m

16. The national flag of the Bahamas is shown at the right. Classify the triangle in the flag by its angle measures.

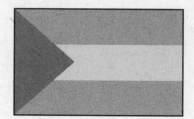

17. A roof truss is used to support the roof of a house. Find the value of *y*.

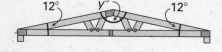
12°   *y*°   12°

Name _____ Date _____

Practice

For use with pages 529–534

Use the clues to sketch and classify the quadrilateral described.

1. This figure has four sides each with length 30 millimeters. Its opposite sides are parallel. Not all of the angles are congruent.

2. This figure's opposite sides are parallel with one side of length 4 centimeters and another side of length 5 centimeters. This figure has four right angles.

Tell whether the figure is a polygon. If it is a polygon, classify it. If it is not, explain why not.

3.

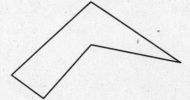

4.

5.

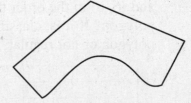

Name _____ Date _____

Practice

For use with pages 529–534

Classify the polygon and tell if it is regular. If it is not regular, explain why not.

6.
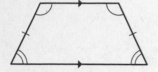

7.
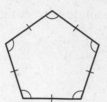

8.

9.
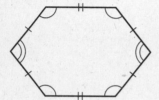

10.
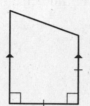

11.
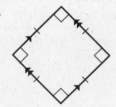

12. Graph and connect the ordered pairs (6, 6), (6, 4), (4, 2), (2, 4), (2, 6), and (6, 6) in the order they are given. Is the figure that results a polygon? If it is, classify it and tell if it is regular. If it is not a polygon or not regular, explain why not.

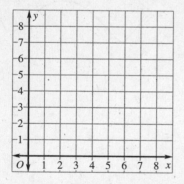

13. The front of the birdhouse shown is a regular pentagon. Find the perimeter of the front of the birdhouse.

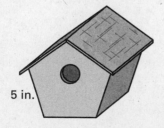

5 in.

14. The stop sign shown is a regular octagon. Find the sum of the angle measures in the stop sign.

10.5 Practice
For use with pages 537–541

Name the corresponding sides and the corresponding angles of the congruent polygons. Then find the unknown measures.

1. $RSTU \cong WXYZ$

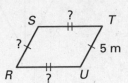

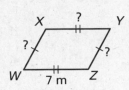

2. $\triangle DEF \cong \triangle GHI$

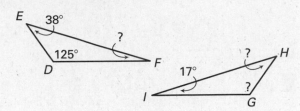

Tell whether the two polygons are similar. If they are similar, find the ratio of the lengths of the corresponding sides of figure A to figure B.

3.

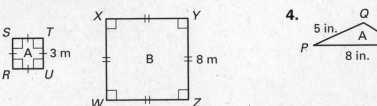

4.

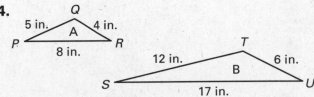

5.

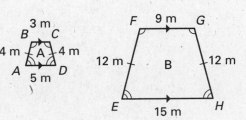

6.

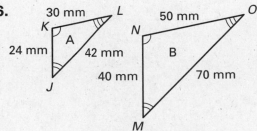

Name _____ Date _____

Practice

For use with pages 537–541

7. A kite is shown in the figure at the right. Name the corresponding sides and the corresponding angles of the congruent triangles △*ABD* and △*CBD*. Then find the unknown measures.

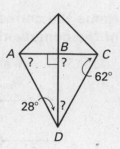

8. The cover of your math book is 11 inches long and 8 inches wide. The cover of your history book is 9 inches long and 7 inches wide. Are the covers similar figures?

Name _____ Date _____

Practice

For use with pages 542–546

1. Describe and correct the error in finding the unknown length x in the similar polygons.

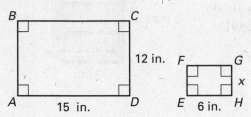

$$\frac{CD}{GH} = \frac{AD}{EH}$$

$$\frac{12}{x} = \frac{6}{15}$$

$$6x = 180$$

$$x = 30$$

Find the unknown length x given that the polygons are similar.

2.

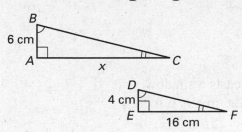

3.

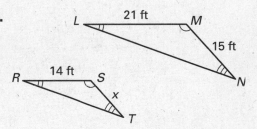

4.

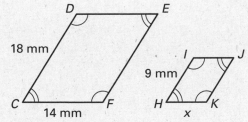

5.

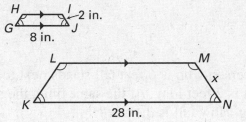

6.

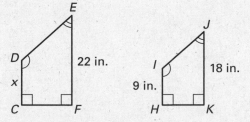

7.

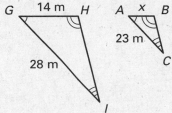

Name _____ Date _____

Practice

For use with pages 542–546

8. You are creating a model of a bookcase for a dollhouse. The actual bookcase is 48 inches tall and 32 inches wide. If you plan to make the model 3 inches tall, how wide do you have to make the model if you want the rectangular shapes of the bookcases to be similar figures?

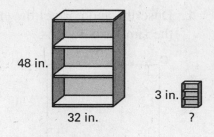

9. A person who is 6 feet tall stands next to a tree and casts a shadow that is 2 feet long. At the same time, the shadow of the tree is 6 feet long. How tall is the tree?

Name _____ Date _____

Practice

For use with pages 548–553

Identify the transformation. If it is a reflection, identify the line of reflection. If it is a rotation, give the angle and direction of rotation.

1.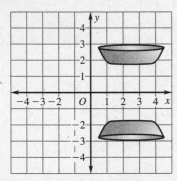

2.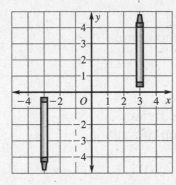

3.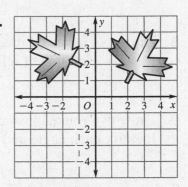

Draw any line(s) of symmetry. Then tell whether the figure has rotational symmetry. If it does, give the angle(s) and direction of rotation.

4.

5.

6.

Name _____ Date _____

Practice

For use with pages 548–553

In Exercises 7–9, use the figure at the right.

7. Draw a translated image of the figure.

8. Draw two reflected images of the figure. Identify each line of reflection.

9. Draw two rotated images of the figure. Identify each angle and direction of rotation.

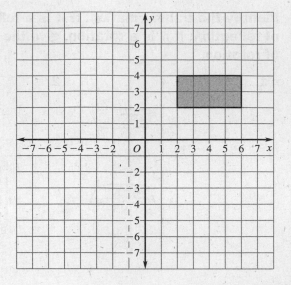

Name _____ Date _____

Practice

For use with pages 556–561

Describe the transformation using coordinate notation.

1.

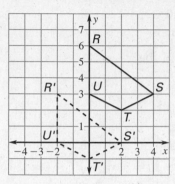

2.

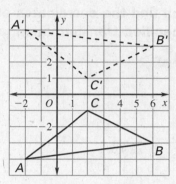

Draw the triangle with the given vertices. Then find the coordinates of the vertices of the image after the specified translation, and draw the image.

3. $P(0, 3), Q(3, 0), R(2, 7)$;
$(x, y) \rightarrow (x + 2, y - 1)$

4. $A(-1, 1), B(3, 0), C(1, -4)$;
$(x, y) \rightarrow (x - 3, y + 3)$

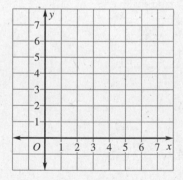

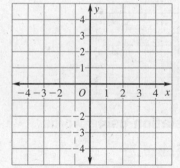

5. $L(-3, -1), M(2, -2), N(3, 1)$;
$(x, y) \rightarrow (x - 4, y - 2)$

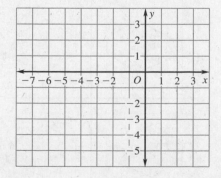

Name _____ Date _____

Practice

For use with pages 556–561

Draw quadrilateral _WXYZ_ with vertices _W_(−3, 0), _X_(1, 3), _Y_(4, 1), and _Z_(2, −4). Then find the coordinates of the vertices of the image after the specified transformation, and draw the image.

6. $(x, y) \rightarrow (x + 1, y - 1)$

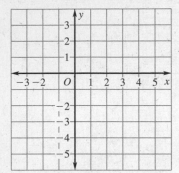

7. Reflect _WXYZ_ in the _x_-axis.

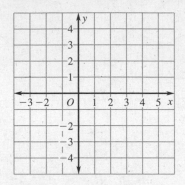

8. $(x, y) \rightarrow (x - 2, y + 3)$

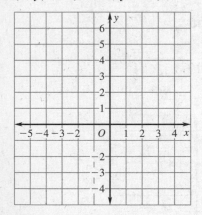

9. Reflect _WXYZ_ in the _y_-axis.

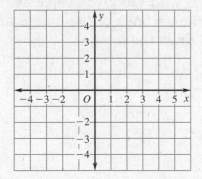

Describe the translation using words.

10. $(x, y) \rightarrow (x - 5, y + 7)$

11. $(x, y) \rightarrow (x + 4, y - 3)$

12. You made the pattern at the right to use as a stencil on a wall. You used three separate transformations of the figure in Quadrant I to make the pattern. Describe the transformations using coordinate notation.

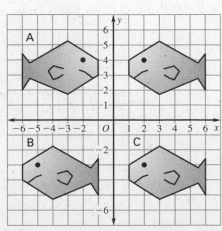

Name _____ Date _____

Practice

For use with pages 577–581

Find the two square roots of the number.

1. 49

2. 400

3. 121

4. 225

5. 3600

6. 576

Evaluate the square root.

7. $\sqrt{900}$

8. $-\sqrt{2500}$

9. $-\sqrt{196}$

10. $\sqrt{324}$

11. $-\sqrt{16}$

12. $\sqrt{784}$

Find the side length of the square with the given area.

13. $A = 4 \text{ m}^2$

14. $A = 25 \text{ in.}^2$

15. $A = 256 \text{ cm}^2$

Evaluate the expression when $x = 2$, $y = 5$, and $z = -1$.

16. $\sqrt{2y + 26}$

17. $\sqrt{-16z}$

18. $\sqrt{95 - xz - 16}$

19. $\sqrt{x^2 + y^2 + 20}$

20. $\sqrt{2x^2 + 1}$

21. $-\sqrt{8z + 44}$

Name _____ Date _____

Practice

For use with pages 577–581

Solve the equation.

22. $a^2 = 169$

23. $3b^2 = 75$

24. $c^2 - 4 = 5$

25. $15 + d^2 = 96$

26. $2x^2 - 7 = 91$

27. $13y^2 = 832$

28. The first, second, and third bases on a baseball field are square canvas bags that each have an area of 225 square inches. What is the side length of a base?

29. When you look at the horizon, the approximate distance from you to the horizon can be found using the equation $d = 370,341\sqrt{h}$, where d is the distance to the horizon, in feet, and h is the height of your eyes above the ground, in feet. Find the approximate distance to the horizon if you are on top of a deck so that your eyes are 16 feet above the ground.

30. A square living room in a home has an area of 110.25 square feet. What is the side length of the living room?

Practice

For use with pages 582–586

Approximate the square root to the nearest whole number and then to the nearest tenth.

1. $\sqrt{27}$ **2.** $\sqrt{92}$ **3.** $\sqrt{130}$

4. $\sqrt{73}$ **5.** $\sqrt{210}$ **6.** $\sqrt{162}$

7. Describe and correct the error in approximating $\sqrt{39}$ to the nearest whole number.

39 falls between 36 and 49. Because 39 is closer to 36, $\sqrt{39} \approx 36$.

Tell whether the number is *rational* or *irrational*. Explain your reasoning.

8. $\sqrt{27}$ **9.** -14.3 **10.** $1.121231234\ldots$

11. $5\frac{2}{3}$ **12.** $\frac{11}{9}$ **13.** $4.\overline{198}$

Approximate the square root to the nearest hundredth.

14. $\sqrt{12}$ **15.** $\sqrt{39}$ **16.** $\sqrt{114}$

Name _____ Date _____

Practice

For use with pages 582–586

Use a number line to order the numbers from least to greatest.

17. $\sqrt{6}, 6, \sqrt{10}, 2.1$ **18.** $2.2, 2.\overline{2}, \sqrt{5}, \frac{5}{3}$ **19.** $\sqrt{33}, \sqrt{35}, 5, \frac{35}{6}, 5.4$

Solve the equation. Round solutions to the nearest hundredth.

20. $5x^2 = 55$ **21.** $8x^2 + 5 = 69$ **22.** $12x^2 = 93.6$

23. You buy 134 square feet of linoleum to cover the floor in a square kitchen. There are 8 square feet of linoleum left over. Approximate the side length of the kitchen to the nearest foot.

24. An A1 sheet of paper has a width of 594 millimeters. The length of an A1 sheet of paper is $\sqrt{2}$ times its width. Approximate the length of an A1 sheet of paper to the nearest millimeter.

25. The maximum speed s, in knots or nautical miles per hour, for a sailboat using wind power can be found using the equation $s = 1.34\sqrt{x}$, where x is the length of the boat's waterline, in feet. What is the maximum speed of a 34-foot sailboat to the nearest knot?

Name _____ Date _____

Practice

For use with pages 588–592

1. Which equation gives the correct relationship between the lengths of the sides of the triangle?

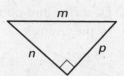

   A. $p^2 = m^2 + n^2$ **B.** $m^2 = n^2 + p^2$

   C. $n^2 = p^2 - m^2$ **D.** $m^2 = n^2 - p^2$

Find the unknown length. Round to the nearest tenth if necessary.

2.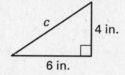

3.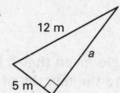

4.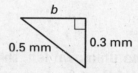

5.

6.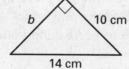

7.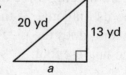

Name _____ Date _____

Practice

For use with pages 588–592

8. Describe and correct the error in finding the unknown length of the triangle.

$$b^2 = 8^2 + 11^2$$
$$b^2 = 64 + 121$$
$$b^2 = 185$$
$$b = \sqrt{185}$$
$$b \approx 13.6$$

The unknown length is about 13.6 meters.

Find the unknown length of a right triangle given that c is the length of the hypotenuse, and a and b are the lengths of the legs. Round to the nearest tenth if necessary.

9. $a = 12$ ft, $b = 15$ ft   **10.** $a = 21$ m, $c = 30$ m   **11.** $b = 20$ cm, $c = 50$ cm

12. You are bracing a rectangular frame by nailing a piece of wood along its diagonal. If the frame is 9 feet long and 5 feet wide, how long does the piece of wood have to be? Round your answer to the nearest foot.

13. You are preparing to clean the windows on the second floor of your house. The windows are 25 feet above the ground and the ladder is 28 feet long. How far away does the ladder have to be from the house so that it is at the bottom of the window? Round your answer to the nearest foot.

Name _____ Date _____

Practice

For use with pages 594–598

Find the perimeter and the area of the parallelogram.

1.
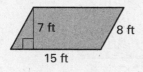

2.
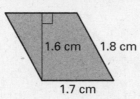

3.
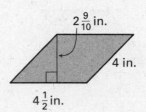

Find the unknown base or height of the parallelogram.

4. $A = 63 \text{ m}^2$, $b = 7$ m, $h =$ _____

5. $A = 180 \text{ yd}^2$, $b =$ _____, $h = 15$ yd

6. $A = 42 \text{ mm}^2$, $b =$ _____, $h = 12$ mm

7. $A = 16 \text{ ft}^2$, $b = \frac{2}{3}$ ft, $h =$ _____

8. Describe and correct the error in finding the area of the parallelogram.

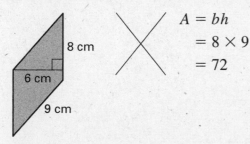

$A = bh$
$= 8 \times 9$
$= 72$

The area of the parallelogram is 72 square centimeters.

Name _____ Date _____

Practice

For use with pages 594–598

Find the height of the rhombus. Then find its perimeter and area.

9.

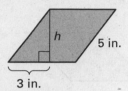

5 in.

3 in.

10.

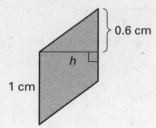

0.6 cm

1 cm

11.

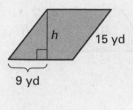

15 yd

9 yd

12. The base and height of a parallelogram in a floor tile pattern are 4.5 inches and 3 inches, respectively. What is the area of the piece of tile?

13. HOV highway lanes are used by vehicles containing multiple passengers. The symbol designating an HOV lane, a rhombus, is shown in the figure. Find the height of the symbol to the nearest hundredth millimeter.

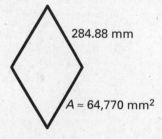

284.88 mm

$A \approx 64{,}770$ mm^2

Name _____ Date _____

Practice

For use with pages 601–606

Find the area of the triangle.

1.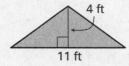
4 ft
11 ft

2.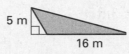
5 m
16 m

3.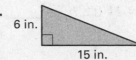
6 in.
15 in.

Find the unknown base or height of the triangle.

4. $A = 56 \text{ km}^2$, $b =$ _____, $h = 8$ km

5. $A = 25.5 \text{ mm}^2$, $b = 3$ mm, $h =$ _____

6. $A = 42 \text{ mi}^2$, $b = 7$ mi, $h =$ _____

7. $A = 88 \text{ ft}^2$, $b =$ _____, $h = 8$ ft

Find the area of the trapezoid.

8.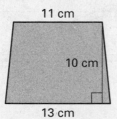
11 cm
10 cm
13 cm

9.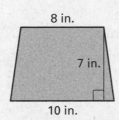
8 in.
7 in.
10 in.

10.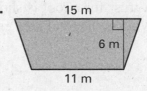
15 m
6 m
11 m

Practice

For use with pages 601–606

Find the unknown base or height of the trapezoid.

11. $A = 21 \text{ ft}^2$, $b_1 = \underline{\hspace{0.5in}}$, $b_2 = 5 \text{ ft}$, $h = 3 \text{ ft}$

12. $A = 10 \text{ cm}^2$, $b_1 = 4 \text{ cm}$, $b_2 = \underline{\hspace{0.5in}}$, $h = 2 \text{ cm}$

13. $A = 44 \text{ in.}^2$, $b_1 = 13 \text{ in.}$, $b_2 = 9 \text{ in.}$, $h = \underline{\hspace{0.5in}}$

14. $A = 91 \text{ m}^2$, $b_1 = 11 \text{ m}$, $b_2 = \underline{\hspace{0.5in}}$, $h = 7 \text{ m}$

15. A truss for a roof is shown in the figure. What is the total area enclosed by the truss?

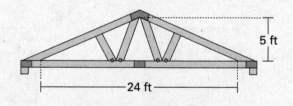

16. A bridge design used for a model railroad is shown in the figure. What is the area enclosed by the trapezoid that makes up the bridge?

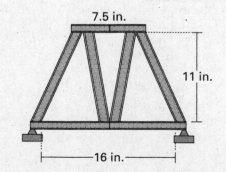

Name _____ Date _____

Practice

For use with pages 607–611

Match the radius or diameter of a circle with the circle's circumference.

1. $r = 16$ in.

2. $d = 8$ in.

3. $r = 8$ in.

A. $C = 8\pi$ in.

B. $C = 16\pi$ in.

C. $C = 32\pi$ in.

Find the circumference of the circle. Use $\frac{22}{7}$ or 3.14 for π.

4.

11 m

5.

9 ft

6.

3.5 cm

7.

24 yd

8.

0.21 mm

9.

15 m

10. Describe and correct the error in finding the circumference of a circle with a radius of 10 meters.

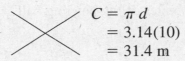

$C = \pi d$
$= 3.14(10)$
$= 31.4$ m

LESSON
11.6
Continued

Name _____ Date _____

Practice

For use with pages 607–611

Find the diameter and the radius of the circle with the given circumference. Use $\frac{22}{7}$ or 3.14 for π.

11. $C = 25.12$ in.

12. $C = 69.08$ m

13. $C = 100.48$ mm

14. $C = 32.97$ km

15. $C = 4\frac{2}{5}$ cm

16. $C = 16.328$ ft

17. Automobile tires are mounted on circular metal rims. If a tire rim has a 13-inch diameter, what is its circumference?

18. Rings are made in sizes that can range from 0 to 13. A size 6 ring has an inside diameter of 16.51 millimeters. What is the inside circumference of the ring?

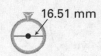

16.51 mm

19. The circumference of a candlepin bowling ball is 14.13 inches. What is the diameter of the bowling ball?

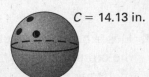

C = 14.13 in.

Name _____ Date _____

Practice

For use with pages 612–616

Find the area of the circle. Use 3.14 for π.

1.
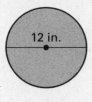
12 in.

2.

5.2 cm

3.

9 yd

4.

32 mm

5.

6.24 ft

6.

15 m

Find the radius and the diameter of the circle with the given area.
Use 3.14 for π.

7. $A = 200.96 \text{ in.}^2$

8. $A = 530.66 \text{ cm}^2$

9. $A = 1256 \text{ ft}^2$

10. $A = 28.26 \text{ m}^2$

11. $A = 1962.5 \text{ yd}^2$

12. $A = 379.94 \text{ mm}^2$

13. Describe and correct the error in finding
the area of a circle with a diameter
of 3.5 inches.

$A = \pi r^2$
$\approx (3.14)(3.5)^2$
$= 38.465 \text{ in.}^2$

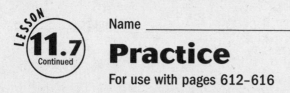

Name _____ Date _____

Practice

For use with pages 612–616

Find the area of the circle with the given circumference. Use 3.14 for π.

14. $C = 31.4$ ft

15. $C = 69.08$ cm

16. $C = 17.27$ yd

Complete the statement using <, >, or =.

17. Area of a circle with a 5 foot radius _____ 75.5 ft^2

18. Area of a circle with a 16 inch diameter _____ 200.75 in.^{2}

19. Area of a circle with a 2.75 centimeter radius _____ 23.74625 cm^2

20. The center ice spot on an ice hockey rink is a circle with a 15-foot radius. What is the area and the circumference of the center ice spot?

21. A dinner plate has an 11-inch diameter and a salad plate has an 8-inch diameter. How many more square inches does the dinner plate cover than the salad plate?

Name _____ Date _____

Practice

For use with pages 631–635

Classify the solid represented by the object. Be as specific as possible.

1.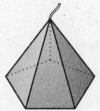

2.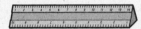

3.

4.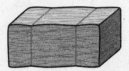

5.

6.

Identify the base(s) of the solid.

7.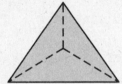

8.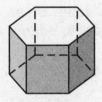

9.

Name _____ Date _____

Practice
For use with pages 631–635

Tell whether the statement is *true* or *false*. If it is false, explain why.

10. A heptagonal pyramid has nine faces.

11. A prism has one base.

12. A pentagonal pyramid has six vertices.

Classify the solid. Be as specific as possible. Then count the number of faces, edges, and vertices in the solid.

13.

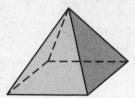

14.

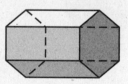

15.

Identify the solid by its description.

16. This solid has one circular base.

17. This solid has two congruent bases, five faces, six vertices, and nine edges.

Name _____ Date _____

Practice

For use with pages 636–639

Sketch the solid.

1. Triangular prism

2. Rectangular pyramid

3. Cylinder

4. Pentagonal pyramid

5. Cone

6. Heptagonal prism

Match the view with its solid.

7. The front view of the solid is a rectangle.

8. The top view of the solid is a square.

9. The front view of the solid is a triangle.

A.

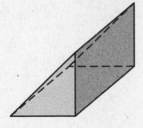

B.

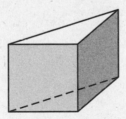

C.

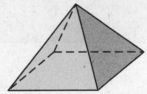

Name _____ Date _____

Practice

For use with pages 636–639

Sketch the top, side, and front views of the solid.

10.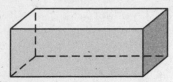

11.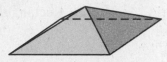

12.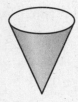

13.

14. Sketch the top, side, and front views of the loaf of bread shown.

15. Sketch the top, side, and front views of the container of oatmeal shown.

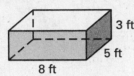
Name _____ Date _____

Practice

For use with pages 642–647

Draw a net for the rectangular prism. Then use the net to find the surface area of the prism.

1.
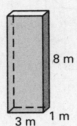
3 ft
5 ft
8 ft

2.
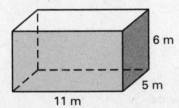
8 m
3 m   1 m

3.
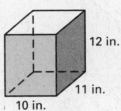
12 in.
11 in.
10 in.

4. Describe and correct the error in finding the surface area of the rectangular prism.

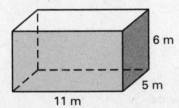
6 m
5 m
11 m

$$S = 11(5) + 11(6) + 5(6)$$
$$= 55 + 66 + 30$$
$$= 151 \text{ m}^2$$

LESSON 12.3 Continued

Name ______________________________ Date __________

Practice

For use with pages 642–647

Find the surface area of the rectangular prism.

5.

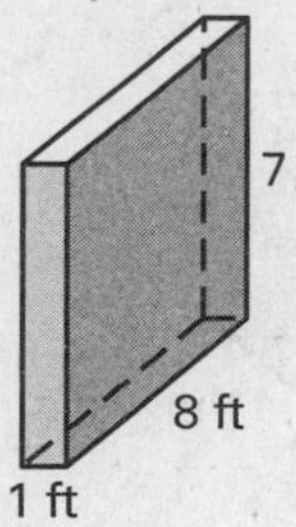
7 ft
8 ft
1 ft

6.

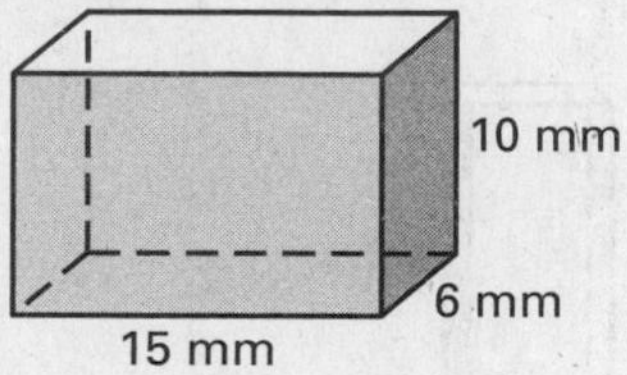
10 mm
6 mm
15 mm

7.

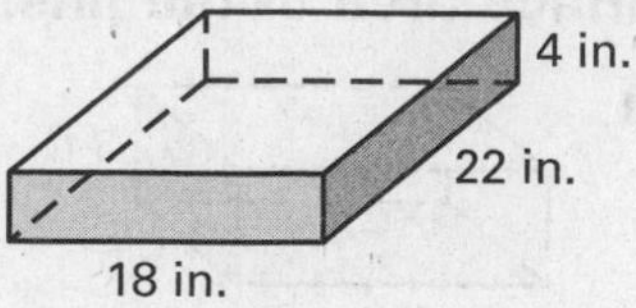
4 in.
22 in.
18 in.

8.

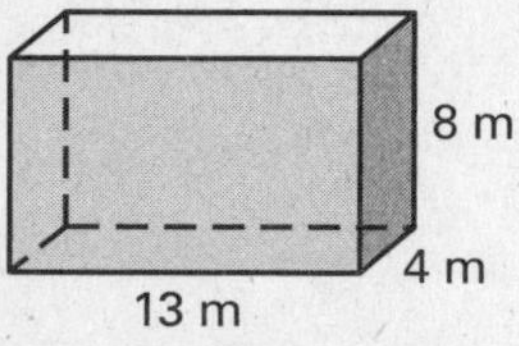
8 m
4 m
13 m

9.

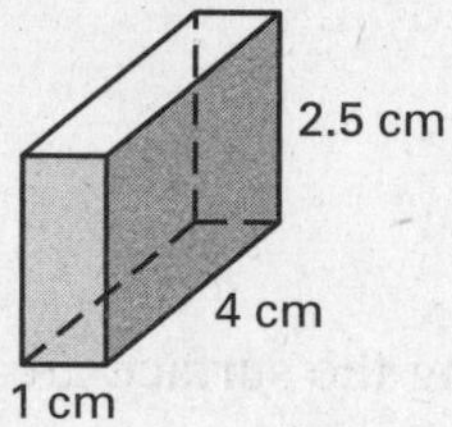
2.5 cm
4 cm
1 cm

10.

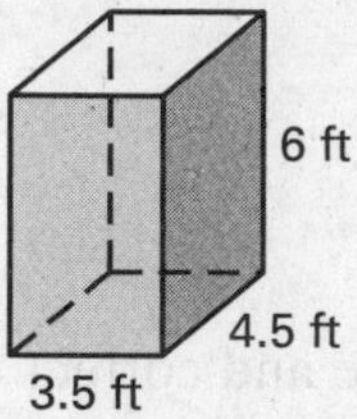
6 ft
4.5 ft
3.5 ft

11. You are wrapping a gift box that is 15 inches long, 12 inches wide, and 4 inches deep. Use a net to find the length and width of a single sheet of paper that could be used to wrap the entire gift box.

12. You are making a set of 12 wooden building blocks for your brother. Six of the blocks will be 2 inches long, 2 inches wide, and 2 inches high. The other six blocks will be 4 inches long, 3 inches wide, and 1 inch high. Find the total surface area of the wooden blocks so you can buy enough paint to cover the blocks.

Name _____ Date _____

Practice

For use with pages 649–653

Draw a net for the cylinder and label the dimensions. Then use the net to find the surface area of the cylinder. Use 3.14 for π.

1.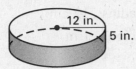
12 in.
5 in.

2.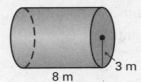
3 m
8 m

3.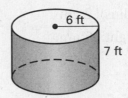
6 ft
7 ft

Find the surface area of the cylindrical object. Use 3.14 for π.

4.
2 in.
BREAD CRUMBS
7 in.

5.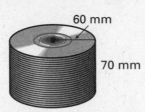
60 mm
70 mm

6.
Pennies
20 mm
75 mm

Find the height of a cylinder with the given radius and surface area. Use 3.14 for π.

7. $r = 4$ m
$S = 251.2$ m^2

8. $r = 10$ in.
$S = 753.6$ in.^{2}

9. $r = 8$ cm
$S = 703.36$ cm^2

Name _____ Date _____

Practice

For use with pages 649–653

Find the surface area of a cylinder with the given dimensions. Use 3.14 for π. Write your answer using the smaller unit.

10. Radius: 2 cm
Height: 5 mm

11. Radius: 3 in.
Height: 4 ft

12. Radius: 12 cm
Height: 1 m

13. You are decorating the hat box shown. If you cover all but the bottom of the box in fabric, how much fabric do you need?

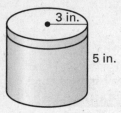
3 in.
5 in.

14. A soup can has a diameter of 80 millimeters and a height of 125 millimeters. What is the surface area of the soup can?

15. A builder is painting the support columns for the front porch of a house before they are installed. There are four columns and they are each 15 feet tall and 4 feet in diameter. How much paint do you need to completely cover all four columns with one coat of paint?

Name _____ Date _____

Practice

For use with pages 655–659

Find the volume of the rectangular prism.

1.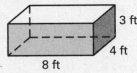

2.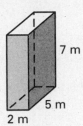

3.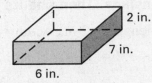

4.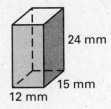

5.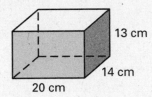

6.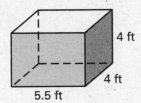

Find the unknown length, width, or height of the rectangular prism.

7. $V = 120 \text{ mm}^3$
   $\ell = 5$ mm
   $w =$ ____
   $h = 3$ mm

8. $V = 720 \text{ ft}^3$
   $\ell = 10$ ft
   $w = 8$ ft
   $h =$ ____

9. $V = 1500 \text{ cm}^3$
   $\ell =$ ____
   $w = 20$ cm
   $h = 5$ cm

Name _____ Date _____

Practice

For use with pages 655–659

Make a sketch of the rectangular prism with the given dimensions. Then find its volume.

10. length = 2 in., width = 2 in., height = 3 in.

11. length = 5 cm, width = 6 cm, height = 7 cm

12. length = 40 mm, width = 45 mm, height = 30 mm

13. Find the volume of the aquarium shown.

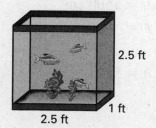

2.5 ft

1 ft

2.5 ft

14. You are building the steps shown below. How many cubic inches of concrete will you need to make the steps?

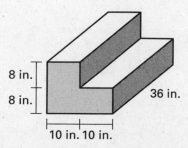

8 in.

8 in.

36 in.

10 in. 10 in.

Name _____ Date _____

Practice

For use with pages 662–666

Find the volume of the cylinder. Use 3.14 for π.

1.

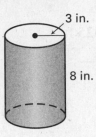

3 in.

8 in.

2.

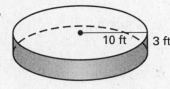

10 ft   3 ft

3.

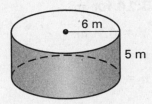

6 m

5 m

4. Describe and correct the error in finding the volume of the cylinder.

7 mm

15 mm

$$V = \pi r^2 h$$
$$\approx (3.14)(7)^2(15)$$
$$= 2307.9 \text{ mm}^3$$

Tell which cylinder has the greater volume.

5. Cylinder A: $r = 5$ ft, $h = 12$ ft; Cylinder B: $r = 7$ ft, $h = 10$ ft

6. Cylinder C: $r = 20$ cm, $h = 15$ cm; Cylinder D: $r = 22$ cm, $h = 14.5$ cm

Name _____ Date _____

Practice

For use with pages 662–666

Find the unknown radius, diameter, or height of the cylinder.
Use 3.14 for π.

7. $V = 628$ in.^{3}

$r = 5$ in.

$h = $ _____

8. $V = 565.2$ m^3

$r = $ _____

$h = 20$ m

9. $V = 3925$ ft^3

$d = $ _____

$h = 50$ ft

10. A swimming pool is 3 feet deep and has a diameter of 12 feet.
How much water would be needed to completely fill the pool?

11. For a hiking trip, you are filling two insulated cylinders with soup.
If one cylinder has a diameter of 5 inches and a height of 9 inches
and the other cylinder has a diameter of 4.5 inches and a height of
12 inches, how much soup can you take for the trip?

12. A cylindrical glass is 13 centimeters tall and has a radius
of 4 centimeters. What is the volume of the glass in cubic
centimeters? What is the volume of the glass in liters if
1 cubic centimeter = 0.001 liter?

Name _____ Date _____

Practice

For use with pages 682–687

Suppose you spin the spinner shown, which is divided into equal parts. Find the probability of the event. Write the probability as a fraction, a decimal, and a percent.

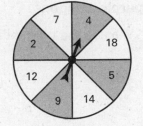

1. Pointer lands on an odd number.

2. Pointer lands on a number that is divisible by 2.

3. Pointer lands on a number that is a multiple of 9.

4. Pointer lands on a prime number.

Each letter in MASSACHUSETTS is written on a separate piece of paper and put into a bag. You randomly choose a piece of paper from the bag. Find the probability of the event. Write the probability as a fraction.

5. You choose a T.   6. You choose an N.

7. You choose an S.   8. You choose an A.

You randomly choose a shape from the shapes below. Find the probability of choosing the given shape. Write the probability as a fraction.

9. Sun   10. Moon   11. Star

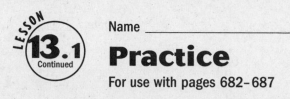

Practice

For use with pages 682–687

**In Exercises 12 and 13, use the following information.
A bag contains 46 blue balloons, 29 red balloons, and
25 purple balloons.**

12. What is the probability that you randomly choose a red balloon?

13. What is the probability that you randomly choose a purple balloon?

**In Exercises 14 and 15, use the following information. In your
backpack, you have a bag where you keep your pens. There are
8 red pens, 3 blue pens, 4 black pens, and 2 green pens in
the bag.**

14. What is the probability that you randomly choose a red pen from
the bag?

15. What is the probability that you randomly choose a blue or black
pen from the bag?

Name _____ Date _____

Practice

For use with pages 690–694

**Make a tree diagram to find the number of
outcomes of the event involving the spinner(s).
Each spinner is divided into equal parts.**

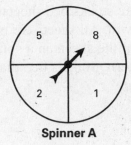 

Spinner A   Spinner B

1. Spin spinner B two times.

2. Spin spinner A and spinner B.

3. Spin spinner A two times.

4. Spin spinner B three times.

5. A buyer is purchasing mailing envelopes for an office. The envelopes
come in white or tan, and come in sizes of 6 inches by 11 inches,
8.5 inches by 11 inches, and 10.5 inches by 15 inches. The buyer
can also choose between unpadded envelopes, padded envelopes, or
bubble-lined envelopes. Make a tree diagram to find all of the
possible envelope combinations.

6. A deli has an option to create your own sandwich. Your bread choices
are white, whole wheat, or rye. You can choose between ham, turkey,
or tuna fish as a sandwich filling and American, cheddar, Swiss, or
provolone as a cheese topping. Make a tree diagram to find all of the
possible sandwich combinations.

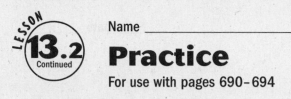

LESSON
13.2
Continued

Name _____ Date _____

Practice

For use with pages 690–694

7. A department store stocks bed sheets that come in four sizes: king, queen, full, and twin. All sheets are made of flannel or cotton, and you can get any of the sheets in a solid color, in a striped pattern, or in a flowered pattern. Make a tree diagram to find all of the possible sheet combinations.

A store sells a grab bag of three travel-sized games. A bag contains one of the following books: a book of crossword puzzles, a book of word searches, or a book of word scrambles. The bag also contains a checkers game or a chess game and one of the following games: a tile game, a board game, or a drawing game. Use a tree diagram to find the probability of the event.

8. A bag will contain the word scramble book.

9. A bag will contain the crossword puzzle book and the drawing game.

Suppose that you roll two number cubes. Use a tree diagram to find the probability of the event.

10. Both numbers are even.

11. You roll a 2 and a 4.

LESSON
13.3 Practice

For use with pages 696–700

Use the number of outcomes of the events to find the number of ways that the events can occur together.

1. **Event A:** 12 outcomes
   Event B: 9 outcomes

2. **Event A:** 5 outcomes
   Event B: 14 outcomes

3. **Event A:** 15 outcomes
   Event B: 20 outcomes

4. **Event A:** 16 outcomes
   Event B: 18 outcomes

5. **Event A:** 11 outcomes
   Event B: 30 outcomes
   Event C: 11 outcomes

6. **Event A:** 25 outcomes
   Event B: 15 outcomes
   Event C: 20 outcomes

7. A clothing store sells a brand of jeans that comes in 3 different colors, 8 different sizes, and 2 different styles. If the store guarantees that it stocks at least one of each pair in each color, size, and style possible, what is the least number of jeans that the store stocks in that brand?

8. You are working on the yearbook staff and are writing up receipts for the presale of the yearbook. If you use a five-digit number to identify each receipt, how many receipts could you write up?

Name _____ Date _____

Practice

For use with pages 696–700

9. You are planning your yearly garden. You've decided that you want
to grow corn, carrots, beans, and tomatoes. In a seed catalog, you find
that you can choose from 5 varieties of corn, 6 varieties of carrots,
8 varieties of beans, and 15 varieties of tomatoes. How many
different vegetable combinations are possible?

10. You roll two number cubes. What is the probability that you roll a
5 and a 2?

11. You are addressing a letter to a friend and realize that you've lost the
zip code. You know that the first two digits are 1 and 4, but you don't
have any idea what the last three digits are. What is the probability
that you choose the correct digits in the correct order from all of the
possible combinations of digits?

12. A painter numbers copies of his paintings with a 4-digit number and
makes enough copies to use up all of the possible 4-digit numbers.
If you buy one of his numbered paintings, what is the probability
that you will buy the painting that is numbered 5142?

174 **McDougal Littell Math, Course 2**
Chapter 13   Practice Workbook

Practice

For use with pages 702–707

Simplify the expression.

1. $9 \times 8 \times 7 \times 6$

2. $\dfrac{14 \times 13 \times 12}{3 \times 2 \times 1}$

3. $\dfrac{15 \times 14 \times 13 \times 12}{4 \times 3 \times 2 \times 1}$

Find the number of permutations.

4. Ways to arrange the letters in the word HISTORY

5. Ways to arrange 6 people in a line

6. Ways to list any three songs from a list of 15 songs

Find the number of combinations.

7. Ways to choose 3 different potatoes from the following kinds:
Russet, Idaho, Red, Yukon Gold, Yellow Finn, Peruvian Blue

8. Ways to choose 4 different books from 15 books

9. Ways to choose 6 different stamps from 24 stamps

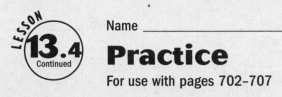

Name _____ Date _____

Practice

For use with pages 702–707

**In Exercises 10–13, tell whether the situation describes a
permutation or a *combination*. Then answer the question.**

10. A teacher is writing up a schedule for oral book reports. For two
    weeks, the class will listen to 3 book reports a day. If there are
    30 people in the class, how many ways can the teacher choose
    3 people for the first day of the reports?

11. You have to run errands on Friday which involves going to 5
    different stores. In how many different orders can you visit the
    5 stores?

12. Your family is planning a movie night. At the video store, you have
    narrowed down your movie choices to 10 movies. You can only
    choose 2 movies for the night. How many ways can you choose the
    2 movies?

13. Your school has assigned a summer reading list. You have to read
    8 books during the summer. How many ways can you order the read-
    ing of the books?

Name _____ Date _____

Practice
For use with pages 709–714

Tell whether the events are *disjoint* or *overlapping*.

1. Event A: A person knows how to skateboard.
   Event B: A person doesn't know how to skateboard.

2. Event A: A person lives in Boston.
   Event B: A person lives in Massachusetts.

3. Event A: A number is less than 10 and odd.
   Event B: A number is divisible by 3.

Events A and B are disjoint events. Find *P*(A or B).

4. $P(A) = 0.32$
    $P(B) = 0.15$

5. $P(A) = 0.18$
    $P(B) = 0.25$

6. $P(A) = 30\%$
    $P(B) = 9\%$

Events A and B are complementary events. Find *P*(A).

7. $P(B) = 0.63$

8. $P(B) = \frac{2}{3}$

9. $P(B) = 92\%$

LESSON 13.5 Continued

Practice

For use with pages 709–714

In Exercises 10–13, use the circle graph that shows the percent of sales for each kind of music at a record store. Find the probability that a randomly chosen person who bought music at the store bought the specified kind of music.

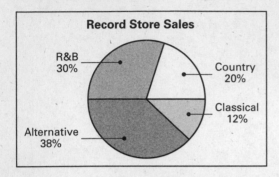

Record Store Sales

R&B 30%
Country 20%
Classical 12%
Alternative 38%

10. Bought R&B or alternative

11. Bought classical or country

12. Didn't buy alternative

13. Didn't buy classical

14. At a dinner, 5 people ordered chicken, 6 people ordered fish, and
12 people ordered vegetable lasagna. A person is randomly chosen
and asked what he or she ordered. What is the probability that the
person ordered chicken or fish?

Name _____ Date _____

Practice

For use with pages 715–721

Tell whether the events are *independent* or *dependent*.

1. You roll a number cube two times. The first time you roll a 2 and the second time you roll a 1.

2. You study 4 hours for your English exam. You get a good grade on the exam.

Events A and B are independent. Find the unknown probability.

3. $P(A) = 0.7$
   $P(B) = 0.2$
   $P(A \text{ and } B) = \_\_\_\_$

4. $P(A) = 0.5$
   $P(B) = \_\_\_\_$
   $P(A \text{ and } B) = 0.15$

5. $P(A) = \_\_\_\_$
   $P(B) = 0.6$
   $P(A \text{ and } B) = 0.48$

Events A and B are dependent. Find the unknown probability.

6. $P(A) = 0.35$
   $P(B \text{ given } A) = 0.6$
   $P(A \text{ and } B) = \_\_\_\_$

7. $P(A) = 0.3$
   $P(B \text{ given } A) = \_\_\_\_$
   $P(A \text{ and } B) = 0.12$

8. $P(A) = \_\_\_\_$
   $P(B \text{ given } A) = 0.2$
   $P(A \text{ and } B) = 0.04$

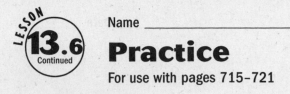
Practice

For use with pages 715–721

Each letter in the word DIVISION is written on a separate piece of paper. You randomly choose letters one at a time, but you do not replace them. Find the probability that both events A and B will occur.

9. **Event A:** The first letter you choose is an I.

   Event B: The second letter you choose is an I.

10. **Event A:** The first letter you choose is a vowel.

    Event B: The second letter you choose is a consonant.

In Exercises 11 and 12, tell whether the situation describes *independent events* or *dependent events*. Then answer the question.

11. A bag contains 18 blue, 24 red, and 30 yellow balloons. You randomly choose a balloon from the bag, but you do not replace it. Then you randomly choose another balloon. What is the probability that both balloons are blue?

12. You have created a computer program that randomly selects a number from 1 to 20. You run the program two times. What is the probability that the program selects 5 as the first number and 7 as the second number?